MEDITATION: THE INNER WAY

Also in this series:

AN INTRODUCTION TO GRAPHOLOGY
Ellen Cameron
COLOUR THERAPY
Mary Anderson
DOWSING
Rodney Davies
HOW TO BE A MEDIUM
J. Donald Walters
HOW TO DEVELOP YOUR ESP
Zak Martin
INCENSE AND CANDLE BURNING
Michael Howard
INVISIBILITY
Steve Richards
LEVITATION
Steve Richards
PRACTICAL VISUALIZATION
Chris Odle
UNDERSTANDING ASTRAL PROJECTION
Anthony Martin
UNDERSTANDING ASTROLOGY
Sasha Fenton
UNDERSTANDING THE CHAKRAS
Peter Rendel
UNDERSTANDING CRYSTALS
Neil Irwin
UNDERSTANDING DREAMS
Nerys Dee
UNDERSTANDING THE I CHING
Tom Riseman
UNDERSTANDING NUMEROLOGY
D. Jason Cooper
UNDERSTANDING PALMISTRY
Mary Anderson
UNDERSTANDING REINCARNATION
J. H. Brennan
UNDERSTANDING RUNES
Michael Howard
UNDERSTANDING TAROT
Jocelyn Almond and Keith Seddon

MEDITATION
THE INNER WAY

How to use meditation as a powerful force for
self-improvement

Naomi Humphrey

Aquarian/Thorsons
An Imprint of HarperCollinsPublishers

The Aquarian Press
An Imprint of HarperCollins*Publishers*
77–85 Fulham Palace Road,
Hammersmith, London W6 8JB

Published by The Aquarian Press 1987
7   9   11   13   15   14   12   10   8

© Naomi Humphrey 1987

Naomi Humphrey asserts the moral right to
be identified as the author of this work

A catalogue record for this book
is available from the British Library

ISBN 0 85030 508 X

Printed in Great Britain by
HarperCollinsManufacturing Glasgow

CONTENTS

Introduction 9

1. What is Meditation? 23
2. Why Meditate? 39
3. The Techniques of Meditation 57
4. Let Meditation Commence 79
5. The Historical Perspective 95
6. Let Meditation Continue 120
7. Inspiration for Meditation 134

Glossary 147
Notes and References 149
Picture References 151
Bibliography 153
Index 157

This book is dedicated with love and thanks to my family for their confidence, to Martin for his patience and to Jerry for his valued help.

PREFACE

This book was written to be both simple and practical; meditation should be both. It should be experienced, not merely read about. The book does not pay homage to a particular system but seeks to show the universal principles upon which meditation is built. Those of a committed faith, as well as those of no particular spiritual persuasion are warmly invited to work through the practical exercises and participate in the inner experience for themselves. The book seeks to engage your active involvement rather than your intellectual curiosity. It offers you experiences which are both gentle and illuminating and gives suggestions for your own future meditative practice. Meditation is lifelong; it does not have to end when the book is finished. Instead let that be the beginning.

INTRODUCTION

Meditation as a way of life is thousands of years old. We find meditation practice in the ancient civilizations of China, India and Africa, and in the younger culture of Europe. We find it in the major religions of Buddhism, Hinduism, Christianity and Islam. It is impossible to say where it began and what form it might have originally taken. Currently it is enjoying a revival in the West. In the 1980s meditation is a word familiar to practically everyone, even if they have never taken up meditation. Yet only a few decades ago the concept of meditation would have been unfamiliar to all but the esoterically minded. Its popularity is, however, curious, for meditation is a discipline which has been transplanted from its spiritual roots. It rightly belongs in the temple, the monastery or the ashram. Yet it has survived the transition to the secular world surprisingly well. Its popularity says a great deal about our own times which are marked by a sense of spiritual malaise.

The practice of meditation is now quite widespread. It is no longer confined to small groups of devotees, but is accessible to anyone wishing to be taught. Weekend courses, seminars and classes are not difficult to find. Meditation is even taught in evening classes, so popular has it become. Some doctors advise patients to meditate daily as a means of dealing with a wide variety of stresses and strains. It is not uncommon to find articles dealing with meditation in popular magazines or hear it discussed on the radio. This is a measure of the interest in the subject. Meditation is not confined to the young and unorthodox at heart as anyone who has attended a meditation group will verify. The young and the not so young, housewives, businessmen, professionals and the unwaged – all share the experience of meditation together. The practice of meditation is open to anyone with the will to learn.

The reasons for the blossoming of this movement in the West are a complicated mix of changing attitude and changing times. It is impossible to say exactly where and when the current revival began. It is not so difficult to see why it has caught on; merely look about: the pace of life is so fast, the demands of life are so stressful and so many old values have fallen by the wayside. Meditation as a way of life has a great deal to offer today's hectic and divided world. It is just as valid today as it was a thousand years ago and as valuable in London as in Khatmandu. The sixties saw the rebirth of a mass quest for spiritual values, predominantly among the young. It was exuberant and vociferous, often seeking to escape from the materialistic values of its elders. The movement certainly created shock waves as it changed mass consciousness. Amidst the slogans and the excesses there was a deeply felt need for a new value system. Out of the melée of the sixties has come a more realistic and stabilized sense of purpose. The flower children have grown up and put down roots. They have handed on the torch to the next generation. Those heady days are over, but the legacy lives on in a more restrained form. The flamboyance and excess have gone but the essential inner spirit is still alive, for which we can all be thankful. The society which loses sight of the quest for meaning and purpose is inwardly dead.

The particular climate of the sixties prompted many to pack their bags and take refuge in the fabled lands of India and Nepal. They hoped to meet a spiritual master on the road and perhaps some did. What they found was a totally new way of life with a different orientation. Many discovered meditation as an integral part of life. Some returned with faith revitalized, carrying new-found treasure to share with others. Others came back disappointed having discovered that the spiritual life is not to be found in the external world but within. Others did not come back at all.

This century has witnessed many changes in thought and knowledge from the scientific and technical to the psychological and metaphysical. Growth psychology has established itself as a valid movement for realizing human potential. We are beginning to understand the importance of personal exploration as a means of releasing creativity and untapped resources.

Over the last few decades there has been an expansion in our understanding of the relationship between mind and matter. This revolution has changed our perceptions about many life experiences and has helped to establish the holistic approach to health and well-being. New medical discoveries have considerably altered our understanding of the mechanisms which create good health. The autonomic nervous system was once thought to be outside conscious control; we now believe that it can be influenced by particular mental states. Psychosomatic illness is no myth; it occurs daily. The mind it seems has the power to create the conditions for either good health or ill health. Psychological health is now thought to be fundamental to physical well-being.

These new realizations lead us to view the ancient art of meditation in a new light. It is after all the oldest form of mental training still in existence. Our previously held mechanistic view of man and the universe has become more subtle and complex, and within this new view there is an important place for meditation.

The atmosphere of the present age is particularly conducive to the spread of meditation. Science no longer mocks the idea of inner states of being. In fact much research has now been carried out into the process of meditation. This in itself is hardly remarkable; yet the recognition that certain states of mind are worthy of investigation represents a landmark in scientific attitudes. The study of the mind as the seat of consciousness can now be taken seriously. Psychedelia has grown up. In addition religious freedom makes it possible to explore new spiritual systems without fear of persecution. Perhaps at no previous time has such opportunity been offered to the individual. Meditation, once the heritage of the minority, has been passed on to everyman. Meditation is for you.

Meditation is an ancient art which has survived outer world change and turmoil over the centuries. It has always attracted those of a certain inner disposition – the introspective, the mystical and the philosophical. In previous ages meditation was generally part of a committed spiritual life that demanded withdrawal from the world, often within a monastic environment. This is no longer the case. The treasures of the meditative life are now open to us through the work of teachers who believe it has become possible to spread knowledge in a different way. There is now no need to abandon the world in order to meditate. The written word now serves as a substitute for the personal teacher. This may or may not be a good thing; ultimately some personal supervision is welcome as the meditative life deepens. However, the general opening up of the subject is a positive step. It should be made simple and accessible. It belongs to everyone.

Meditation has emerged into an age which has all but overthrown its own spiritual heritage. The vacuum created by this loss has served to redirect personal energies back into the search for spiritual values. Paradoxically many who have vigorously thrown off the traditional yoke take up the discipline of meditation quite happily. What is it that meditation has to offer? Why does it still appeal in the twentieth century? What is the value of techniques first used by Buddhist monks, Christian hermits, Zen roshis and Sufi masters? What does meditation have to offer the individual and the wider group? The Tibetan teacher who wrote extensively through the hand of Alice Bailey made it perfectly clear that meditation should be seen as a force for world transformation.[1] This is indeed a staggering claim but it is also an inspiring one, for the world is certainly in need of transformation. The Tibetan outlines the concept of a network created by illuminated minds around the globe together acting as a force for good within mass consciousness. If we take up meditation we probably expect personal results of some kind. We do not expect to change the world – or do we? The ripples that spread out from a simple act of meditation may not be immediately apparent. Members of the TM movement have been especially interested in the wider effects of meditation. They claim that crime, acts of violence and other anti-social behaviour decline as the number of meditators increase in the community. It is suggested moreover that there is actually a critical turning point within group consciousness when meditation becomes a positive and dynamic force for good.

Some support for this argument is given by what has been called the case of the hundredth monkey.[2] It is based on the behaviour of a group of monkeys on a Japanese island. By chance one monkey discovered that potatoes dipped in sea water were better to eat. She was observed teaching this to others in her group until it was common behaviour. The same behaviour then spontaneously appeared among members of the same species on other islands. Such monkeys had no contact whatsoever with the original band. The phenomenon is not easy to explain. The hypothesis put forward suggests that when new behaviour is integrated into the group it is more likely that others will also discover and adopt it for themselves. It is suggested that every person who takes up meditation makes it easier and indeed more likely that someone else quite unknown to them will also be able to do the same. The idea of critical mass is important in the natural world. We know that evolution can suddenly take an unexpected leap. Circumstance and prior development interact and combine in a unique way. Out of this comes a jumping-off point. It gives rise to a radical new line of development. Perhaps we are close to a quantum leap in mass consciousness? Who is to say what the critical number might be in the case of meditation? Perhaps *you* might be the 'hundredth monkey', the one that makes all the difference.

Meditation and the Brain

A casual observer walking into a meditation session might wonder what if anything was actually happening behind the closed eyes and calm exteriors. What happens in the mind/brain during meditation is fundamental to our understanding of the process. How are we able to gather information in this seemingly impenetrable area? We have on the one hand the personal accounts of individuals both ancient and modern to draw upon. Subjective opinion, however, has never found favour with scientific thinking and the meditation experience is bound to be a highly personal one. Until recently the subjective account remained our only source of information. However, the unlikely field of electroencephalography has provided us with some important clues into the mechanics of the process. It was in the early twenties that Hans Berger made the discovery that the brain is in a constant state of electrical activity which might be recorded through the strategic placing of electrodes on the scalp. He was abused and ridiculed for his claims, but in time they became the foundation for a brand new field of medical research and knowledge. This branch of science has moved on considerably since the early pioneering days. It has proved invaluable in the diagnosing of brain abnormalities such as clots, tumours and epileptic fits, all of which give unusual brain patterns. It has also been put to other uses. Commencing in the 1950s the EEG machine has been used to monitor the brain waves of subjects using various systems of meditation.

The field of electroencephalography has considerably expanded our understanding of the mechanics of the mind. Perhaps the most interesting of these new findings is the discovery of four brain waves, each eliciting a different frequency range of electrical activity. They have been called the Alpha, Beta, Delta and Theta rhythms respectively. Of these the Delta rhythm is the slowest, giving a reading of between 0.5 and 4 HZ, cycles per second. Not surprisingly this slow wave is most commonly associated with deep sleep. The Theta rhythm is normally defined as having a frequency range of between 4 and 7 HZ. It usually appears in the dream state but not in great abundance. The Alpha rhythm which has proved to be the most interesting and the most controversial, gives a reading of 8–13 HZ. It appears most easily when the eyes are closed and the subject is relaxed. It seems to be associated with a clear waiting mind and a state of relaxed wakefulness. Finally the Beta rhythm registers at 13–30 HZ. It is found most frequently in the normal waking state and is associated with active attention, solving concrete problems and with being externally focused. The discovery of these four brain patterns provides a new dimension to our comprehension of the brain's complex functions.

The question that naturally poses itself at this point is a very simple one. What is the correlation between the meditative state and the electrical activity of the brain? The answer unfortunately is not as simple as the question, even though we are now sure that there *is* a correlation. Early research seemed to equate the meditative state solely with the appearance of the Alpha rhythm.[3] This has proved to be too simplistic even though the Alpha wave remains significantly indicated in the studies so far. There are many techniques of meditation. Complex Tibetan meditation for example primarily uses a visual technique which creates quite a different experience from TM. Different types of meditation are in all probability going to produce different electrical patterns. Results may also be affected by the experience of the subjects and their own training in meditation itself. So the question cannot simply be answered by observing large numbers of subjects meditating while attached to EEG machines. Studies so far have revealed the increasingly complex nature of the interrelationship. Early research found enhanced Alpha activity with Zen meditation. Later studies have surprisingly observed the appearance of activity within the Beta range, which is normally associated with intense problem-solving, during Zen and yogic meditations. One very thorough study by Das, a famous electroencephalographer, and Gastaut, a neurophysiologist, monitored the physical and mental changes taking place in an advanced yogic meditation.[4] Initially there was an increase in the Alpha rhythm, followed by the appearance of

Beta, culminating in activity around the 30–50 HZ range which has not yet even been given a name. Following this intense period of absorption, Alpha reappeared as the meditation period came to a close. The complexity of this reading indicates something of the difficulty which investigators face. It would seem to be beyond doubt that different states of mind are reflected in different forms of electrical activity within the brain but these are not in a static relationship, moving constantly in response to the specific form of mental process. Visual meditations will elicit a different response from non-visual ones while the states of bliss, rapture and joy which accompany deep meditational experiences have as yet no physically recognized counterpart. This form of investigation is still in its infancy. Researchers still have much to learn from advanced practitioners. Such trained minds have on numerous occasions produced readings which outstrip present understanding. However, it remains a potentially fruitful field which has served to establish the basic fact that meditation produces quite distinct and remarkable changes in the activity of the brain.

The Alpha rhythm has drawn particular interest as it appears on its own or with other patterns in almost every study. Researchers have become interested in the effects of sustaining the Alpha rhythm alone. The Alpha rhythm appears when the individual is relaxed and calm. It is found more frequently when the eyes are closed, but with practice it can also be produced with the eyes open. It coincides with a mental state which is described as being free from judgements, tranquil and has the feeling of letting go. This state resembles certain meditational states and describes the preparatory phase in the meditation process itself. The vast majority of people enter this state of mind quite spontaneously though usually for only short periods. Alpha training sessions have been used to teach people to recognize, sustain and then apply this specific mental state. Training programmes invariably use monitoring devices of various kinds which instantly feed back information to the subject. The constant flow of information enables the subject to observe minute physical or mental changes and thereby recognize and sustain the particular state. This process is known as biofeedback.

Alpha training programmes have been developed which have focused upon the process of self-awareness or else they have been developed as pilot studies into the effects of this state of mind on various clinical problems. Alpha training sessions have been used with patients suffering from a wide variety of disorders, including alcoholism, addiction, chronic pain, psychiatric disorders and epilepsy.[5] The results over a wide range of symptoms have been very encouraging. It is interesting that training programmes are built around the twin concepts of mental relaxation and creative visualization, which also form the foundation for so much meditational experience. It can only be hoped that research will continue to throw more light onto the complex relationship between mind and body.

Brainwave biofeedback offers new possibilities in the area of health and well-being which might be more completely realized in the future. The work of Maxwell Cade, Nona Coxhead and Geoffrey Blundell has already shown how brainwave biofeedback can be used as a guiding principle in the area of personal growth and self-understanding.[6] Their combined work marries traditional meditation techniques with the most sophisticated of monitoring devices – the Mind Mirror. This machine gives an instantaneous and easily comprehended display of the brain activity in both hemispheres together with information showing the different brain patterns. The display consists of two banks of light-emitting diodes set side by side, with twelve rows to each bank. Each bank records the activity of one hemisphere through the twelve separate frequency channels. In practice electrodes placed on the scalp pick up the electrical signals from the brain which are then translated into a light display. The signals appear on the twin banks. The subject is able to watch the results of thought processes in rapidly changing configurations and to observe the subtle effects that different states of mind create. The Mind Mirror is probably the most sophisticated monitoring device to date. It has shown that the altered states of mind which characterize meditation are a physiological reality. Training sessions teach people how to recognize and produce certain states of mind in both the physical and psychological sense.

One of the most interesting findings to emerge from research with the Mind Mirror concerns the different activity of each hemisphere of the brain. The existence of the two hemispheres has been known for a long time but it is only recently that we are beginning to appreciate the significance of this fact. We now know that the function of each hemisphere is quite different. The left hemisphere is concerned with language, logical thought, deductive reasoning, and all the rational forms of thinking. The right hemisphere is concerned with image creation, shape and pattern recognition, symbolic understanding, abstract and intuitive thinking. Our society in general, and education in particular, places great emphasis on the qualities that are expressed through the left hemisphere. We tend to devalue non-verbal thinking, distrust the imagination and be suspicious of subjective experience. Our society encourages and indeed rewards activity that reflects this particular bias. This unbalanced development has even appeared in the most literal sense on the Mind Mirror as an asymmetrical pattern expressing dominance of the left hemisphere over the right. This configuration is characteristically found in people who find it difficult to let go and explore any inner feelings. It is significant that this asymmetrical pattern becomes transformed into a symmetrical configuration as experience in meditation practice is gained. Meditation has the power to awaken areas of mind long dormant. Mystical literature speaks of the search for wholeness and here we see a concrete example of it.

We find ourselves at a unique moment in time. Meditation techniques have been used for centuries around the globe but it is only recently that technology has given us a rare insight into the mechanics of the process. Scientific enquiry is the standard Western approach to almost any question. It seems to encapsulate the Western outlook on the world. We need to understand the process before we feel able to commit ourselves to it; we feel the need to explore intellectually before we feel able to experience personally; we need to prove to ourselves that something will be worth doing before we can act. Scientific results are interesting in their own right and research will add to the body of knowledge. However, even when we understand the mechanics of the process we cannot claim to know any more than that. The mystery of meditation remains and cannot be explored by scientific method. It can only be experienced.

Meditation and the Mind

Western science has provided us with an enhanced understanding of the mechanisms by which certain meditational techniques operate. It is important to remember however that we are unable to answer all the questions posed by the process of meditation by simply observing changes at the physical level. We do not expect to understand the artistry of a dancer by purely measuring muscular change. We do not expect to comprehend what it means to be a great athlete by solely monitoring bodily reactions. We cannot expect to appreciate the full significance of meditation by confining ourselves to observing the brain at work. We need a theory of mind to guide us. It is at this point that Western psychology, still in its infancy, reaches a cul-de-sac. Other psychological systems far older than our own are more willing to offer teaching on the subject of mind. What might prove to be impossible terrain for the Western psychologist is familiar territory to the Zen roshi, Hindu guru or Buddhist teacher.

Any theory of consciousness will in many ways reflect the prevailing cultural philosophy. Current Western materialism invariably equates consciousness with brain function. Hindu philosophy starts from a quite different spiritual perspective. All matter is thought of as a manifestation of spiritual reality. It is the result of the outpouring of spiritual force. Consciousness is immanent within form. Consciousness is universal not particular. Hindu philosophy suggests the existence of different levels of consciousness or mind which become increasingly dense as manifestation proceeds. Each level has its own qualities and universal functions. The higher and more refined levels permit abstract mental functions and the denser levels carry instinctive drives and memory functions. The individual mind is like a single wave in the ocean. It cannot be considered as isolated and self-contained. The personal mind is but a part of the whole. Each individual partakes in different levels of mind through a series of sheaths or vehicles of consciousness. These are sometimes depicted as a series of interpenetrating luminous forms which surround and interact with the physical being. Expansion of the personal mind brings these more subtle vehicles into conscious use. It is presumably possible for a Hindu adept to use a higher vehicle much as the man in the street uses the physical body.

Buddhist psychology also offers us an alternative model of mind and matter. Accordingly, the universe itself is nothing but consciousness. It is divided into nine levels. The first six are the root consciousness of seeing, of hearing, of smelling, of tasting, of touching and of thinking. These six together comprise individual consciousness which is born and dies. The seventh, eighth and ninth levels do not perish upon death. The seventh level is the consciousness of self-awareness. The eighth level, relative *alaya* consciousness receives all the sense data gathered at the first six levels. It is gathered here and recorded moment after moment. These impressions in turn seed the next action, to set in motion a constant cycle of activity. The ninth level, absolute *alaya* consciousness is the pure formless self consciousness of the True-nature. There is little difference between these two levels.

The state of enlightenment occurs when there is a conscious breakthrough into all the levels of consciousness at once. Such models are radically different from current Western psychology. Both models offer fully integrated theories of consciousness. Psychology and cosmology are not separated.

In the West we invariably associate the mind with the intellect. We associate a sharp mind with intellectual activity, a keen mind with intellectual prowess. We place a great deal of value on the rational use of the intellect. We use the term 'irrational' almost as an insult. It carries the implication that an inferior form of thinking is at work. We save the highest accolade for the trained intellect, for the mind which has acquired knowledge by learning about things, usually in an ordered and systematic way, through a long process of education. We do not really recognize the value of any other form of thinking. Eastern philosophy places limitations on the value of the intellectual processes. Reason has its place but eventually it will reach a point beyond which it cannot go without changing radically in form. A higher function will come into operation which knows directly. It bypasses the intellectual reasoning process. It is called *prajna*, that is wisdom. In Tibetan the equivalent term is *sherab*, meaning higher knowledge. The nearest Western equivalent is intuition or intuitive knowledge. If we changed 'intuition' to 'inner tuition' we might come closer to understanding this higher function of ourselves. Hindu teaching also carries a distinction between *avidya* which is partial knowledge, and *vidya*, which is complete knowing. Vidya is based on direct perception of the underlying unity of all things. As consciousness evolves so avidya is transformed into vidya. Such concepts are probably new to the average Westerner. They are worthy of reflection. These distinctions can help prepare the individual to leave the safe realm of the intellect for the new and uncharted waters of direct knowing, of intuition. Such a leap can be challenging and transforming. It becomes possible to move on from knowing about something to knowing something directly. We may happen to know a great deal about the cultivation of apples. We might know how to look after the tree, how to protect it and ensure a good crop. We might know the names of many types of apples and how each has been derived. We might know all of this and a great deal more besides without ever tasting an apple for ourselves. In real life we confuse knowing about the apple with tasting it. We mistake knowing *about* something for knowing something itself.

Zen places much emphasis on 'right seeing', which means seeing things as they really are, stripped of any projections that we might place on them. This is seeing with the eye of Wisdom without distortion or interference. When we recognize something for its own special qualities without elaboration we perceive the 'suchness' of the object in view. It is a direct perception which is razor-sharp and immediate. It is a form of comprehension quite unlike that which we are used to. The higher mind will develop slowly and with use. It is bolder and richer than the deductive form of thinking which is bound to follow certain rules. It is expansive yet keenly focused, for all that is superfluous is recognized as such. It is a creative level of mind for it is aware and open. It is a level of mind which knows but has no need to hold on to knowledge, for insight is ever-present in every situation. Such is the meditational mind; constantly alive, ever awake.

Hermetic philosophy represents the mind by the symbol of air. It is invisible, all-pervading, and life-giving. It reminds us of the difficulty in working actively in this area. It gives us a clue if we should seek to explore our own minds. When we wish to use and control the power of air, we confine it within a space. When we wish to use and control the power of the mind we must confine it within a space; this is meditation.

It is difficult enough to grasp the nature of the personal mind. It is quite impossible to grasp the nature of the Divine Mind. Sacred texts universally recognize this fact. We are lead towards the comtemplation of a prime creative source through symbol, allegory, parable or other representation. Metaphysical philosophy has always recognized a dilemma: what can man really say about the nature of God? We can know nothing except indirectly through creation and perhaps through the lives of those we come to accept as mediators.

In Hindu philosophy the absolute source of creation is called Brahman. The word is derived from a root which means 'to expand'. This prime reality is described as having two aspects. The first is called the Supreme Brahman. It is beyond all comprehension. The Supreme Brahman is designated only by what is not, 'Neti, Neti', 'Not this, Not this'. The Inferior Brahman is described as He 'whose body is spirit, whose form is light, whose thoughts are true.'[7] The two levels are part of the same reality. The Qabalah offers similar teaching. The absolute level of reality is referred to as Kether. It can be symbolized by the image of an ancient bearded King in profile. We only see one side of the face. In the same way, we can never see the dark side of the moon but we know it exists. We also know that the Absolute exists.

Meditation in its highest form is intimately connected with the relationship between the individual mind and a greater mind. Christianity, Sufism and Hinduism perceive this greater mind in terms of a Godhead, Buddhism in terms of a Void. This term can be confusing to the Western faithful who have been brought up with the idea of a personal Godhead. The concept of *sunyata* reminds us that we can know nothing of this level of reality and cannot presume to do so. It does not carry the usual meaning of emptiness, for in Buddhist thought, 'Form is Emptyness, Emptyness is Form.' Such riddles are beloved by Eastern philosophy.

Paradox stops us in our tracks and makes us think in a new way. Both schools of thought envisage a return to a state which is unknowable yet essentially real. The goal of every spiritual path is to touch, no matter how briefly, the greater level of reality and to consciously merge mind into Mind. This is the real quest of the meditational path.

CHAPTER 1

WHAT IS MEDITATION?

It is possible to define meditation in many ways, each being valid. It is only natural to seek to understand something through a definition of terms but in this case specific definitions may serve to restrict rather than illuminate. Words can serve to obscure meaning rather than reveal it. Chuang-tzu, a Taoist sage of the fourth century said 'Words exist for meaning, but once you understand the meaning you can throw away the words.'[8] You may each come to your own definitions and conclusions as experience becomes your teacher. It is impossible to convey the reality of meditation through words alone. Meditation can only be known through experience. It can only be comprehended when it is lived. It cannot be understood intellectually any more than an understanding of love can be felt from reading romantic fiction, or a subtle taste explained to someone who has never experienced it. Armchair reading never made an athlete, or an artist, a driver or a bricklayer. Learning about meditation is no more than a preparation for experience. It is not a substitute. To know meditation is to live meditation. It can be helpful, however, to liken meditation to various concepts that already hold meaning for us. In this way we can open ourselves to new experiences. We can see meditation as a state of consciousness or a way of life. We might see meditation as the path to enlightenment and a spiritual discipline. We might see meditation as a psychological process and a means of becoming more aware. There is no reason why meditation should not include all these concepts and more besides. Such ideas can be helpful when they serve to expand our thinking, not limit it. It is more valuable however if we use intellectual structures only as signposts and permit the inner journey itself to inform us of its nature.

Meditation as a
State of Consciousness

It is obvious that meditation is a mental activity which concerns our own consciousness. In this sense consciousness has nothing to do with intellectual prowess, educational background or mental aptitude. It can be thought of as pure perception or total awareness. It is quite distinct from thinking about something in an intellectual manner. We have become so used to the intellectual approach that it is at first difficult to envisage any other mode. When we think about something we quite naturally view it as the object of our thinking. We always place a space between ourselves and the object. We learn about something by absorbing certain facts from which we are able to draw conclusions. Our judgements are often limited by the information available to us. Inadequate or faulty information leads to wrong or poor judgements. The rational and logical action need have no moral or ethical base as such considerations are not part of this process. If we look at any history book we will find countless examples of inhumane but logical actions.

When something is only the object of our thinking it is somehow lessened in value and placed outside ourselves. When we come to know something through meditation we have done so through direct perception in which we have shared an experience as part of the 'object' of our thinking. We do not attempt to learn about something but to understand the nature of something itself. If for example we were to take the simple concept of a tree as a meditation subject for a while we might experience something of its life cycle, its relationship to the sun, to the air, to water and to the earth. We might share the feeling of being host to a mass of smaller life forms. We might come to know the sensation of the rise and fall of the sap and even to feel the slow accretion of annual growth. We might touch upon its longevity and even go on to experience different tree forms and various leaf structures. Such realizations create permanent changes in consciousness which also inform behaviour and judgement. Who could remain oblivious to the consequences of the destruction of woodland on perfectly logical economic grounds having shared in the life cycle of the tree itself? Through meditation we have come to know the tree, not just to know about the tree.

Direct involvement through conscious participation creates a quite different interaction with all life experiences. Some people intuitively understand the degree of loss that a purely intellectual

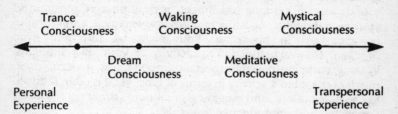

Figure 1

approach carries with it and feel like bystanders watching life through an inpenetrable window. They observe life happening all round them but feel cut off from the pulse of it. Meditation uses direct perception as its *modus operandi*. It is not what we have been used to. It is a new form of consciousness for most of us.

We regularly utilize several different forms of consciousness. We each quite naturally and spontaneously switch levels of conscious awareness from being outwardly focused to being inwardly focused throughout the day from moment to moment. This is a perfectly natural adaptation to surroundings and circumstances rather like the constant adaptation made by the pupil of the eye to the source of light. We each move through a range of possible levels of awareness. We might arrange these for our convenience as a spectrum (see figure 1). These states are not separate but flow into one another quite naturally. We do not even normally notice the process taking place. Meditation, however, brings even this into conscious awareness so that an option opens to us.

We might like to begin to think about meditation by first turning our attention to our everyday waking consciousness, which is familiar territory for each of us. It is after all the seedbed from which the meditational mind will arise. Waking consciousness is a particular and highly specialized adaptation of mind which has evolved over many thousands of years. It has evolved to suit a particular need, namely to deal effectively with the external environment. Waking consciousness has its own particular qualities which we may each observe in ourselves if we should wish. Primarily we think about things outside ourselves, whether the focus of our thoughts be another person, an event or a task in hand. We may not even realize it but thinking is fragmented and scattered. Images arise and fall instantaneously. Thoughts rush from one subject to another. There is little continuity of mind; instead there is a rapidly flowing stream of consciousness. If this sounds like an extreme indictment, merely observe the train of your own thoughts for a few minutes and experience this form of consciousness in operation. You might be surprised, even shocked, to watch the darting activity of your own thoughts. Waking consciousness is especially important as it occupies so much of the mind's activity in terms of time, yet it is often reduced to a purposeless and seemingly random stream of loosely connected and unproductive thoughts.

We alternate between waking and sleeping. We spend about one third of our lives asleep. During sleep, consciousness is busily involved in the process of dream creation. Everyone at some point has experienced powerful or frightening dreams. These will continue to exert a fascination until they are resolved. Like the biblical Pharoah whose prophetic dreams were interpreted by Joseph, we each seek an interpretation which will give us peace. Dreams emerge from a part of the mind which is not under conscious control, hence their mysterious and irrational quality. Nevertheless they form an important and even vital aspect of our minds. Whether remembered or not, they are an important active factor in our mental well-being. Dream deprivation brings serious psychological disturbance. It is interesting to observe that regular meditation creates changes within dream life, effectively making it more coherent and organized so that it serves as an extension of consciousness. The metaphysical writers Rudolf Steiner and Alice Bailey both suggest that the awakened individual seeks continuity of consciousness in both states, so that the whole of life becomes one continuous flow. This is perhaps rarely achieved but it cannot be thought of as an impossible goal. For the majority, however, the time spent dreaming is time lost. Yet we are still able to recognize that the dream consciousness is real and part of our experience of life.

We are each familiar with the qualities and characteristics of both dream and waking consciousness. We are perhaps less familiar with a third possible state of consciousness, that of trance. For many this state carries unacceptable connotations and arouses fear. Yet it too is a naturally occurring state which we have each experienced in a light form without knowing. When we become so engrossed in a book that we do not notice the passing of time or when we find a film so moving that we weep as the tragedy unfolds we have internally created a lightly entranced state. Our singleness of concentration and fixity of attention are the dominant features of trance. We have in fact hypnotized ourselves by entering into the reality of an imagined scenario and experiencing it within ourselves. This may come as something of a shock to many who express a natural aversion to the very idea of trance. Yet the fact remains that we have followed exactly the same stages that are used specifically to induce trance under more controlled conditions. The trance state is deepened as awareness is focused upon an increasingly reduced area. The classic induction technique which uses hand or arm levitation serves to focus the mind upon a very limited area of response. This simply eliminates the normal flow of random and scattered thoughts which divert concentration. The trance state can be created by any trigger which serves to focus attention. It could be visual, auditory or kinaesthetic.

The trance state offers some important therapeutic possibilities and should not be devalued. The body seems able to reduce the awareness of pain if the suggestion is given in a state of trance. The mind also seems able to access distant and long-forgotten memories which may be at the root of psychological disturbance. The trance state is still a form of consciousness not fully understood. It is a perfectly natural state of consciousness in which awareness is inwardly focused. It can vary from a light and briefly experienced trance to a deep somnambulistic state. At this deeper level it might superficially be seen to resemble the withdrawn state of profound meditation. However, the two states should not be confused. They are quite different. Deep trance invariably results in loss of recall for the time period and very often the individual is dependent on the guiding technique of an operator. Newcomers to the practice of meditation often expect to experience a similar state. This is not the case. The trance state in its various degrees is natural and has its uses on occasion. However, deep trance should not be confused with deep meditation. Meditation brings neither loss of recall nor loss of personal awareness. The mind is active not passive, the mental faculties are being expanded not diminished. Trance and meditational consciousness are diametrically opposed even though there is a superficial resemblance; and some literature is confusing on this point.

There are many states of consciousness which occur quite

naturally. Each has its own characteristics and qualities. Yet each is also part of a whole spectrum of consciousness. Waking consciousness is characterized by its fragmented nature. It is a level of awareness in which we communicate with others and deal with the external environment in an often highly superficial way. It is, however, a level of shared mind and communication. Dream consciousness is extremely personal, and its images are often strange and difficult to understand. The mind seems to be looking inwards in a way which we cannot control. The consciousness of trance is characterized by a narrowed focus of awareness. The mind is limited to a very restricted area of personal consciousness. It is not a level of mind that can be shared or even sustained for any length of time. Each of these states represents an increasingly personal and diminished level of awareness. The meditative state on the other hand brings about an expansion of consciousness. It, too, has its own characteristic qualities. It is different from the waking state; the mental process is continuous and sustained. It is different from the dream state; the images are consciously created and the process is controlled. It is different from the trance state as consciousness is not lost or diminished but expanded and sensitized. Yet meditation can be thought of as an altered state of consciousness. It is entered in a particular way and when the state is completed there is a return to waking consciousness. In the beginning meditational practice seems to be quite different from the consciousness of our everyday lives. We tend to regard practice as being something set apart from our everyday lives, almost like a short visit to a desirable place. With time this distinction fades as practice begins to alter the very nature of everyday consciousness itself. Eventually meditation becomes a way of life, not just a particular state of consciousness.

Within the meditative state there are certain landmarks which express the degree of mental involvement and the form of experience which may take place. In Buddhist terminology the deepening levels of concentration are called *jhanas*. At the outset of practice the mind wanders quickly and is easily distracted. This is a stage we are all familiar with. Onepointedness is occasional and easily disrupted. With practice the mind remains focused for longer periods and even when distracted is easily returned to the focus point. In the early stages certain obstacles appear to be almost insurmountable. We can be plagued by self-doubt and lack of confidence. Inertia and mental laziness weigh heavily upon our shoulders. With persistence and determination we make progress until we are able to observe our powers of concentration improving. There will come a point when concentration shifts from focusing on the object of the meditation to becoming one with it. This is considered to be a state of absorption and marks entry into the first jhana. When this happens there are no interruptions to concentration. The experience of effortless concentration may be only fleeting but with practice it becomes stabilized. When this level of absorption has been mastered it becomes possible to deepen the experience further by mentally moving into the second jhana. This is done by commencing with the set subject for the first level and then deliberately turning away from it towards bliss, rapture and deepened onepointedness. These states of mind bring an intense joy. They are used as inner rungs in the ladder of mental concentration. To reach the next level the meditator passes through the experiences of the previous level, abandoning the qualities of each stage. At the fourth level the pleasurable sensations of bliss and rapture give way to equanimity and absorption. The fifth level marks a turning point. The subject for meditation is now totally abstract and without form, infinite space. The mind enters a formless experience. The mind is absorbed into the experience of infinite space. At the next level the mind experiences infinite awareness. At the seventh level the focusing point is the non-existence of infinite awareness. At the eighth and final level the mind experiences 'neither perception nor non-perception'. All mental activity is stilled. Even the physical metabolism is radically altered so that the body is almost in a state of suspension. It is difficult to comprehend what is meant by these descriptions. Such experiences are not easily attained and would certainly require close personal supervision. We may even ask ourselves the relevance and value of such experiences in our lives. This particular path develops the power of concentration to an extreme point, probably to its very limit. It is a system of mind training which has little to offer the layman of today. Concentration may be fundamental to all meditative practices but the intensity and abstraction of these levels is beyond any ordinary needs. Historically this system is of interest as it points the way to states of consciousness which even now remain a mystery.

The path of concentration is always considered to be secondary to the higher path of insight. The path of concentration ends in the achievement of the eighth level but the path of insight ends in

Nirvana. This path also has its landmarks. It commences with the practice of mindfulness. This practice aims to break preconceived responses and habituated behaviour. Through mindfulness we come to see every moment with clarity and accuracy. When mindfulness is continuous it matures into insight; seeing every minute event as it truly is, not through the veil of personal interpretation. The focus of meditation is the experience of life at every moment. The meditator comes to experience the renewal implicit in every moment and the impermanence of all phenomena including the self. When the illusion of the permanent self is faced and understood the way is considered to be open to the higher realizations which may finally culminate in the state of Nirvana. This is too often misunderstood to mean an after death state or a state of total extinction. It is neither. At first the touching of the Nirvanic state may be only momentary. It is said to be a deeply shattering experience for it is here that the silence of the Void is glimpsed. All the illusions finally fall away. There is only the certain experience of Reality.

The spiritual path brings transformation at every step. Ultimately it can bring a final transformation, but only when individually we truly seek and totally desire to face the ultimate mystery.

Meditation is most often regarded as being a particular event which takes place in the setting of daily life. However, it should never be seen as only that which takes place in the time allotted for meditation practice. The experience of meditation will infuse the whole of day-to-day living so that it becomes possible to see meditation as an act of being rather than as an event or even a process. It becomes inseparable from the whole life experience. It becomes a level of awareness which penetrates all activities, thoughts and decisions so that every aspect of being expresses the meditational state.

Meditation as a Spiritual Way of Life

When meditation has become integrated into the pattern of daily life it becomes a natural part of day-to-day living, like washing on rising. It ceases to be a mere exercise or the experience of an altered state of consciousness. Meditation has the power to transform all aspects of individual living; thinking, feeling, doing and knowing. It plants the seeds for enlightenment and becomes a way of life; more than that, it is a spiritual way of life.

We should not forget that meditation has grown up as part of the total spiritual environment of the monastic life. As such it is a practice which is part of a total philosophy. Buddhist meditation is part of Buddhist philosophy. Hindu meditation is part of Hindu teachings, and Sufi meditation is an aspect of Islam. If we attempt to secularize the practice of meditation we reduce it to mental calisthenics. Modern-day Western life is in no way comparable to the timeless pace of regulated and disciplined monastic life. Yet meditation still has a great deal to offer us. Perhaps it is of especial importance to the West today as our own spiritual tradition is undergoing a period of change and uncertainty.

The impact of regular meditation will be felt throughout all areas of daily life like ripples spreading through a pool. It will affect our actions, decisions and total behaviour in the world. It should come as no surprise to discover that meditation brings its own ethical and moral codes of conduct. It cannot be otherwise; when we seek to know ourselves truly we take responsibility for everything that we create and effect. Meditation has the power to transform personal life by placing it in the bright light of spiritual principle. Taking up the practice is therefore not an easy matter. Traditional systems of training lay much stress on readiness for meditation in order to emphasize its central transformative role. The Yoga Sutras lay down requirements for the Hindu wishing to take up meditation. These requirements constitute a code of conduct and ethics. The individual is asked to observe Yama, that is, the laws of life: non-violence, truthfulness, integrity, chastity and non-attachment to worldly things. This is followed by Niyama, the rules for living, which are: simplicity, contentment, purification, refinement and surrender to the Lord. Buddhist monks are subject to a wide range of prohibitions and even laity who take up practice are asked to follow a code of abstentions. It is perhaps unfortunate that since courses in meditation are now more widely available through evening classes or other such arrangements, we tend to view it in the same light as photography or creative writing; as a constructive and hopefully helpful pastime. Such courses perhaps lay insufficient stress on readiness for practice. We might each benefit by drawing up a code of our own desired conduct and ethical behaviour as a preparation for practice and deeply consider why we seek meditation at all. Idle curiosity or intellectual interest are of little use in this instance. Meditation is not a pastime which can be picked up and put down as whim dictates. It is a personal commitment to the goal of enlightenment, liberation or illumination. Taking up meditation in seriousness is a positive and conscious movement towards self-realization. It is this that marks meditation out as a fully fledged spiritual discipline and not just a system of mind-training.

The state of meditation is often referred to as an awakened state. This definition implies that by contrast our normal waking state is in effect one of sleep. This notion may seem ridiculous even insulting to many whose lives are both busy and active. Yet even dreams can be filled with activity. Indeed the paradoxical idea that we sleep while we live is worth dwelling upon. What is it that we should wake up to? What is it that enlightenment will bring us? What is it that keeps us sleeping so soundly? A tale told by Plato illustrates our condition so well. Men are imprisoned in a cave since childhood. Their necks are fastened so that they may only look ahead. Others project images of reality onto a screen, which are taken for reality itself by the prisoners. Plato asks us to consider the possibilities should a prisoner be released.[9] We each face that same choice and frequently we prefer the safety and familiarity of the cave. There is also a pertinent Buddhist tale about a frog and a tortoise. A frog lived in a pond. He had never travelled beyond the confines of the pond so he knew of nothing else. One day a tortoise came by and told the frog that he had come from the ocean. The frog had not heard of the ocean and wondered if it was like the pond. The tortoise explained that the ocean was something like the pond but three times bigger. At this the frog fainted away quite unable to grasp such dimensions. Like the prisoners in the cave and the frog in the pond we also have difficulty in grasping new horizons of experience and being. We are bound by fear of the unknown, unwillingness to change, group pressure to conform and inability to trust. Such is our condition; we dwell in limitation, we live in ignorance and exist in chains that we are too afraid to remove. The world outside the cave and the ocean are not unlike the enlightened state, immeasurably greater, totally different and painful to reach. Many have no desire whatsoever to travel the tortuous path towards enlightenment. The individual with a genuine thirst for enlightenment is driven by an unremitting and powerful compulsion. It is not a passive and intellectual curiosity that drives a person to seek his or her own True-nature but a total and dynamic force.

The practice of meditation gradually enables us to remove our chains, to step away from our fears, transcend our condition and move out willingly into the light of day. It offers us a new way of life which is illuminated from within by its own light. It offers us a spiritual way of life in exchange for our old existence. It is a mistake to think that the spiritual life has to be set aside and apart from the material life. Spirit and matter are not separated but conjoined. We can lead a spiritual life in the world when it is a life guided by indwelling spiritual principles and not dictated by convenient and self-centred interests. We transform the quality of our own lives as we consciously acknowledge our place in the whole and become attuned to the principles and patterns of life itself. The spiritual life is one that is created around conscious participation in the flow and rhythm of universal patterns. It is not a life built around religious platitudes and dogma that have lost their meaning. It is through meditation that we will discover the workings and reality of principles that we can live by. Meditation will by its very nature throw light into the three darkest areas of our existence; namely ourselves, the world about us and an ultimate or absolute level of reality. It brings us face to face with the fundamental questions of our own existence which we cannot evade in the space of our own minds. In Zen it is said that the quickest way to awakening is to struggle with a 'doubt-mass', a perplexing problem which ceaselessly seek resolution. The Zen *koan* is designed to precipitate such a doubt-mass and create the conditions in which enlightenment will break through. Meditation is not for those who prefer the security of the cave for it will become the key to inner awakening and the cornerstone for the spiritual life.

Within the awakened experience of life there is a profound sense of freedom and openness. This comes about as a result of changes in personal perspective and self-image. Our lives are a reflection of our self-image. When we change one we also change the other. It should be no surprise to find that the key phrase, 'Man know thyself' appears in Hindu, Buddhist and Western teachings. Self-awareness, self-knowledge and self-realization are the triple aspects to this vital key. Self-awareness, which comes about through constant mindfulness of thought and deed shows us the effects that we create about us. Self-knowledge, which grows as meditation puts us in touch with deep feelings and inner strengths, brings certainty, direction and purpose. Self-realization brings true confidence and provides us with a glimpse of our own potential. It shows us what it means to be human. Such personal qualities are surely to be valued in a time which seems increasingly discordant and fraught. When we are without self-awareness we fall prey to deception and the unceasing demands of the ego, when we are without self-knowledge we blame others for our mistakes and when we are without self-realization we are incomplete and partial expressions of ourselves. In this state we experience confusion rather than clarity, disorientation rather than purpose. Life may be exceedingly busy and industrious but have we found meaning within it? Have we faced any of life's fundamental paradoxes and found an answer that quietens the mind? We are still asleep and do not even know it.

Life is so often filled with fears of one kind or another. It is the great enemy to equanimity and inner poise. Fear cannot be countered by intellectual means; this does little more than give it a name and identity. We can, however, work with it through meditation and begin to loosen its hold over us. Fear takes many forms; inability to change, holding on to people, possessions or even circumstances so that we only feel secure in our present position. Buddhism teaches that life is constantly changing and flowing. Permanence is illusory; when we seek to create permanence we are merely compounding our ignorance. Meditation on the universal reality of change can provide profound insights into how we should regard each experience and moment, for it will never come again. Life is constantly moving and changing. When we truly recognize the impermanence of all phenomena we are willing and more able to make the most of each experience in our lives. When we are able to observe the flow of life, we cease to cling to external props for security. Time can become our ally rather than our adversary when we harness ourselves to the natural rhythms and work within them. Experience can become our teacher only when we are open to what is happening about us. When we are able to move easily with the flow of our lives we no longer fear change and present resistance to it. It is not always easy to face up to the realities of life, the illusion is often gentler. It is often difficult to accept the ultimate impermanence of our own lives. Death is perhaps the greatest fear of all, yet it remains the only certainty in life. It is a certainty that we are very unwilling to face. In Tibet and in certain Indian schools it was customary for students to attend burial grounds and meditate there among the corpses on this inevitable aspect of life. This may seem very grim to us in our neat and tidy culture, where there seems to be almost a conspiracy to deny that death is part of life, but the purpose should be crystal clear – namely to put us in touch with our deepest fear. We perhaps feel something of this if we attend a funeral, which has the effect of reminding us of our own passing. Our usual reaction is to leave as soon as possible for the place of death always makes us feel uncomfortable. In avoiding our fears and feelings we deny ourselves the possibility of transforming them. When the fear of death has been faced a great liberation becomes possible. Never again will we feel fear and panic at the thought of passing for we have already faced what the experience means for us. Such a task is not easy for our fears are very deep rooted and are tied up with our sense of identity and being. Meditation upon death as both a personal and impersonal reality is a regular aspect of several systems of spiritual training. Do not be afraid to meditate on your own death. There is much to be learned about life in this. There is much to be gained in being free from old fears. We continually evade the lessons that death has to teach. Its lessons are straightforward and powerful. Life is to be treasured and experienced consciously; people are to be valued and loved for one day they will depart.

Meditation unlike intellectual thinking has the power to put us in touch with ourselves. It actively unites our consciousness and creates a sense of personal wholeness which is so often lacking. This sense of completeness becomes a firm foundation which we may build upon. As our sense of self-identity changes we are able to encompass new horizons. Roshi Philip Kapleau, the director of the Zen centre at Rochester, New York, points out that although concern with the self is valid at an early stage in spiritual training it is no more than a night's lodging on the way to true self-realization. Paradoxically self-realization brings deep concern and compassion for the suffering of others. How after all can the enlightened mind ignore the plight of humanity which continues to suffer. In Zen it is said that 'Without enlightening others there is no self-enlightenment.' When Buddha was enlightened he chose out of his great compassion to devote the rest of his life to teaching and laying out a path that others could also tread and reach enlightenment. This original act of compassion established a lofty principle in Buddhist practice and gave birth to the notion of the Bodhissatva as one who serves others from a state of enlightenment. An earthly Bodhissatva is one who has gained enlightenment in the world and serves all living things through an all-embracing compassion, choosing to be reborn again and again to help all beings attain Buddhahood. A transcendent Bodhissatva is one who at the moment of death chooses to dwell in a non-human, other-worldly state from which it is possible to assist in the welfare of mankind. Together they are called the Great Beings or Mahasattava. The idea that an individual is able to awaken and thereby make a conscious choice to remain and serve humanity from a discarnate state is not only found in Buddhism but in each major spiritual system. Such a concept is both humbling and staggering. Perhaps it too is worthy of deep reflection. The Bodhissatva is the perfect embodiment of the enlightened state and the model for every Buddhist disciple, much as Christ might be taken as an ideal example by a Christian. The path towards becoming a Bodhissatva is outlined in ten phases, each increasingly more selfless and compassionate. Here perhaps we are beginning to glimpse the true fruits of self-realization. The Bodhissatva takes four solemn vows which reaffirm that having made a dedication to those in need there will be no turning back. These vows are awesome in their intent and affirm the desire to offer up all personal merit, worth and knowledge for the good of others. According to Santideva, a seventh-century Buddhist thinker, these vows are as follows. We find them in his *Bodhicharyavatara* in the following form:

1. The sin accumulated in my former existences, accumulated in all creatures is infinite and omnipotent. By what powers can it be conquered if not by the desire of Bodhi, by the desire to become Buddha for the salvation of men? This totally disinterested desire is infinitely sacred. It covers a multitude of sins. It assures happiness during the round of existences. It is a pledge of the supreme happiness of the Buddhas for oneself and one's neighbour. All honour to the Buddhas whom everybody naturally loves and who have as their sole aim the salvation of men.
2. I worship the Buddhas and the Bodhisattvas with a view to undertaking the vow of Bodhi. Possessing nothing, by reason of my own sin, how can I render unto them the worship which is their due? But I am wrong. I do possess something. I give myself unreservedly by pure affection to the Buddhas and to their sons, the divine Bodhissatvas. I am their

slave and as such, have no more danger to fear. Of all the
dangers the greatest is that which comes from my sins. I
know how harmful these are; I deplore them; I acknowledge
them. I see and you see them as they are, pardon me.

3. But enough of myself. Let me belong entirely to the
Buddhas and to creatures. I rejoice in the good actions,
which among ordinary men for a time prevent evil rebirths. I
rejoice in the deliverance gained by the Arhats. I delight in
the state of Buddha and Bodhissatvahood possessed by the
Protector of the World. I entreat the Buddhas to preach the
law of salvation of the world. I entreat them to delay their
entrance into Nirvana. All the merits acquired by my worship
of the Buddhas, my taking refuge, my confession of my sins I
apply to the good of creatures and to the attainment of
Bodhi.

4. I wish to be bread for those who are hungry, drink for
those who are thirsty. I give myself, all that I am and shall be
in my future existences, to all creatures. In the same
disposition as those in which the former Buddhas were when
they undertook the vow of Bodhi and just as they carried out
the obligations of the future Buddhas, I conceive the desire
for Bodhi for the salvation of the world. So also I shall
practice in their order my obligations.

The Four Great Vows of a Bodhissatva form the most widely
recited chant in Mahayana Buddhism:

> All beings, without number, I vow to liberate.
> Endless blind passions, I vow to uproot.
> Dharma gates beyond measure, I vow to penetrate.
> The Great Way of Buddha, I vow to attain.

Such vows are taken literally and chanted with intent as
meditations in their own right by Buddhist disciples in many
places. This tells us a great deal about the nature of the self-realized
state. It is a condition which encompasses all living things in its
vision. We may find it impossible to imagine what an enlightened
state might bring and we might not even seek it for ourselves. Yet
we are permitted a glimpse of it in the lives of the spiritual teachers
of mankind. We invariably find the qualities of radiating love, total
compassion and certainty of purpose. Such lives also bear the
hallmark of long years of inner awakening through meditation and

contemplative practice. Who will choose to shoulder such spiritual responsibility, for in all honesty, we wish to awaken gently. Perhaps we should be grateful that others have awakened before us and on our behalf.

Meditation will inevitably bring change in its wake. We will grow and be changed by our realizations. We will become more able to shoulder our small burdens and strong enough to carry increasingly greater ones. We will become more open to the wisdom of the heart and more receptive to the power of insight. Our lives will take on a new quality. We will find depth and perception entering into our experiences. Life will take on an intensity and value that perhaps we had missed before and were unable to find. Meditation will gradually transform every aspect of being and recreate it in a new pattern. Who can say what shape the adventure will take? We only know that it will happen as we stir within our slumber and prepare to awaken in the fullness of time.

CHAPTER 2

WHY MEDITATE?

At first sight this looks like a simple question which deserves a simple answer. If you were to ask one hundred regular meditators you would in all probability receive one hundred different answers. Such answers might range from the down-to-earth, 'I feel better in myself', to the mystical, 'It brings me closer to God'. Perhaps the question is for you to answer in your own time. Meditation is really a personal search and no one person may answer for another.

Meditation may be thought of as a journey, an adventure into the depths of your own being. It is said in Buddhism that we study Buddhism in order to study ourselves. It is a long journey. There is much to discover, more than you ever dreamed possible. It has been wisely said, 'A man would search for God. Let him beware he will discover his true self. A man would seek himself. Let him beware he is in mortal peril of beholding God.' Here is perhaps the first paradox of the search; we look for the self only to lose it, we seek the lesser but find the greater. We begin with the self – after all what else is there that you can truly claim as your own? The injunction to 'Know Thyself' is the universal call to awakening. Perhaps you think that you already know yourself well enough. What, then, is the point in taking up meditation? Look again. Look into the mirror of the self. How well do you know the face that looks back at you and all that lies behind it? What do you really know of your own motives, desires and aspirations? Where have you come from, where are you going? When did you begin and when shall you end? Who are you? What you think, feel and know of yourself at present constitutes the starting point for your journey.

Meditation is a way of change. It is a process of gradual refinement, of distillation and tranformation. It is you who sets the pace for your own progress. It is you who determine whether meditation works or not. Like anything else that is worthwhile meditation requires hard work and discipline. It is not an easy road, for you are transforming yourself at all levels of being by your own application and labour. It is not an easy task but it brings a rich reward. For the sake of simplicity, we may look at the several areas in which meditation may have an impact. In reality this separation does not exist, as meditation itself will certainly reveal. Analysis can usefully precede synthesis on occasion. It is merely helpful to look at the different areas in turn.

Meditation and Physical Well-Being

It is very likely that few of us are as healthy as we should be. Our existing environment is beset by circumstances which actively work against our good health. We generally eat without sufficient care and rely too much on convenience and instant foods. We take insufficient exercise and excessively indulge many destructive habits. Even the air we breathe is impure. We are subject to many work pressures, a heavy schedule, a demanding boss or a difficult colleague. There are always pressures at home, worries about children, relatives, financial worries and anxiety about the future generally. Close relationships have their own particular problems and stresses. In fact we are all pulled from pillar to post. All of these pressures and many more besides go to create a nation suffering from a bewildering array of complaints. Has meditation anything to offer?

Meditation is a conscious act. It might be thought of as the creation of a personal inner sanctuary to which you are able to retreat. Meditation involves deep physical relaxation and the creation of a quite different mental state. It allows you to step outside the pressures of work, home and relationships. For a short time you are able to leave the worries of the daily round elsewhere. If meditation is practised regularly a new and quite different inner perspective begins to establish itself. The outside pressures may not change but your view of them shifts. A new view of yourself begins slowly to form. You discover a stronger more definite sense of self which participates in all the worldly dealings but also stands outside them. Perhaps you also begin to see others in a different light. The boss who was making your life unbearable no longer seems so intimidating. You now perceive him or her in a very different light, just as you are beginning to see everything in a new light. You begin to sense new values forming within yourself and you notice changes taking place in your behaviour. You find that you are calmer, more relaxed, less tense and more able to cope with new situations. Those about you may even remark on the recent changes that have come over you. What others cannot perceive, however, are the subtle physiological changes that are beginning to take place within the body. Each time that you experience deep relaxation you create certain conditions within the mind and body. The mind is alert yet the body is relaxed. Respiration alters; it becomes slower, deeper and more rhythmic. The pulse rate tends to slow and muscular activity decreases. The body is perfectly still, a unique experience for even in sleep the body is extremely active. Oxygen is used at a lowered rate and carbon dioxide is produced at a lower rate. The lactate concentration of the blood, which is closely linked to the anxiety level decreases sharply during meditation. Each time that you enter the meditative state you establish a physiological pattern which acts as a blueprint to which the body can return even in the normal waking state. In time the physiological characteristics of the meditational state extend more and more into our daily lives so that we are relaxed and calm as we go about our daily tasks.

It was long thought that the functions of the autonomic nervous system were quite beyond any conscious control. However it has now been shown that with specialized biofeedback training some functions can be altered. Biofeedback training works upon a very simple principle, namely that the individual requires a constant source of information in order to modify any piece of behaviour. Information from these senses enables us to interact successfully with our surroundings. Biofeedback training merely provides highly specialized information about the conditions prevailing within the body through different kinds of monitoring devices. These feed back a constant source of information to the individual concerning localized body temperature, muscle relaxation or the electrical resistance of the skin for example. It is important to realize, however, that these devices do no more than measure the changes taking place within certain body systems. In this way it is possible to alter muscle activity, body temperature, breathing and even heart rate. Biofeedback training actually shows us how particular states of mind have a real impact on the body. It uses the techniques of relaxation and creative visualization which are also the identical means of training the mind through meditation. Stories have long been told concerning the extraordinary feats of gurus and yogis who have achieved total mastery over the body's functions through the force of the mind alone. We do not need to emulate the singleness of purpose of such men whose entire lives are spent actively exploring the relationships between mind, body and spirit. Perhaps we can at least learn that the mind can affect the body and begin to act upon it in our own lives.

The meditative state of mind affects the body directly by setting up physiological changes and indirectly through creating a sense of inner equilibrium. As awareness of self changes so attitudes towards the body invariably change. Paradoxically the physical body becomes both more and less significant. As self-identification changes so the body seems less permanent and more transient while it also becomes worthy of a heightened respect and care as an aspect of self. Contemporary medical opinion recognizes the fact that the mind can have a powerful impact upon the body and we can see this easily enough for ourselves. As yet neither science nor medicine can fully explain exactly how this relationship functions. According to the metaphysical sciences, however, the transmitting intermediary between the mind and the body consists of a subtle energy field which surrounds and interpenetrates all living tissue. These living yet subtle energies take the form of flowing currents and particular energy centres. If the balance of these living forces become blocked, disturbed or impaired in any way then a corresponding imbalance will appear within the physical body. If the balance is not restored then a complaint, mild or serious, will eventually follow. Unfortunately the West has lost its traditional teachings in this area but in the East specialized knowledge of the subtle energies has been preserved in particular forms of yoga and also through the science of acupuncture. A recent and important development originally pioneered in Russia now enables us to capture the image of the living energy field and study its nature through scientific method. Kirlian photography is possibly an unheralded milestone in our understanding of the subtle energies. We are no longer dependent on subjective studies for information. It is significant that the studies so far confirm the ancient teachings and uphold the power of the mind as a major factor in causing observable change in the energy field. Violent emotional or mental turbulence creates severe disturbance within the subtle centres. A calm, serene and loving state of mind returns the system to a state of equilibrium. Here are important lessons for us as we go about our daily lives.[12]

Physical disease is often prefigured for many years by mental turbulence of one kind or another. The physical symptoms which eventually manifest merely mirror the inner state of mind. It is obvious that there will always be a variety of complex factors at work behind the appearance of illness and some of them will be outside any form of personal control. Certain environmental and genetic factors will continue to cause ill health and disease, but we are able to help ourselves considerably by creating the right mental conditions for physical well-being.

The value of relaxation and meditation has been practically tested as part of the recovery programme with several forms of illness, notably cancer. This approach places some degree of responsibility with the individual and involves the patient in self-awareness through meditative techniques, relaxation and creative imagery. The inner power of the mind can be used not only in a preventive regime but also in a curative programme. Here, too, is an important lesson that we can use in our daily lives.

Physical well-being and better health generally may be a worthwhile bonus to be gained by taking up regular meditation. However, it is important to remember that meditation was not created to work purely at the physical level. Meditation is a spiritual system which caters for the whole being and touches the physical aspect as part of the wider whole. Take up meditation and observe the changes for yourself.

Meditation and Emotional Well-Being

Physical and emotional well-being are closely connected; each seems to reflect the other to some degree. We also tend to take them both for granted – that is, until they are gone. Emotional well-being is a state of mind in which we are able to cope with the problems of our daily lives without feeling unduly beset or harassed by them. We are able to maintain a balanced outlook and keep our feet on the ground. We are on an even keel. We have time for others in our lives, offering them love and affection. In return we feel nourished and supported by their care for us. We have a proportionate sense of our own worth, neither feeling ourselves to be inferior nor in any way superior to others. We treat ourselves and our endeavors with respect, accepting challenge as part of life's pattern. We are not at the mercy of other people's opinions of us. We have sufficient self-esteem to feel inwardly confident. We are not plagued by feelings of guilt, anxiety or self-created fears. We are able to express our feelings naturally and freely. We have respect for the feelings of others and try to treat them as we would like to be treated by them.

Emotional stability and balance is not a given condition that comes with physical maturity. It is slowly won through the circumstances of our lives. We each need to come to emotional maturity or we will forever be dependent on others. As a nation we still seem to fear the emotional side of our make-up, preferring a rational and intellectual approach to life. The display of emotion is often taken as a sign of weakness and men are still brought up to repress the visible show of feelings. This is a particularly unhealthy attitude which refuses to acknowledge the validity of a natural human expression. It is the capacity for feeling deeply one for another that binds us together, man to woman, parent to child, friend to friend. Without our emotions we would be empty robots each self-absorbed in our own little world. Our emotional nature enables us to experience compassion for other living beings and to translate this feeling into positive action. Far from denying the emotional nature we need to recognize and value what it has to teach us.

We have all at some time or another experienced the grip of a powerful emotion. We have each been overwhelmed by grief, filled with passion or consumed with love or even hate. Such deep feelings tend to take us over completely, obliterating everything else in our thoughts. We become swamped by the intensity of the emotion. We seem to be at its mercy and powerless against its force. How should we deal with the emotional part of ourselves? Repressing an emotion is rather like trying to force the lid down on to a boiling kettle. We all know what we feel like when we have to bottle up something just like that boiling kettle, a mass of seething emotion. We only really feel better when the inner tension has been released. If we consciously repress our feelings, ignoring our responses, we do ourselves less than justice as people. On the other hand is it wise to allow our emotional responses to take us over? How do we keep to the middle way? What has meditation to offer us?

Meditation is a process of change, of inner realization and personal transformation which works upon each of the different aspects of being. Within the calmness of the stilled mind the individual is able to begin the process of self-observation, watching thoughts, feelings and behaviour as if they belonged to someone else. Self-observation is one of the major principles of the meditation process. It marks the first step to self-knowledge. Such objectivity is often very difficult to attain. We each have such cherished notions of our own worth and value believing we are always right. This process of self-evaluation does not take place through critical self-analysis or psychological examination, but merely through the simple act of self-observation, often termed 'mindfulness'. The concept of being mindful of oneself is found throughout the major meditation systems. It is regarded as a necessary step on the path of self-knowledge.

In Buddhism there are four approaches to mindfulness each identical in function but different in focus. Mindfulness can focus on the body, on the feelings, on the states of mind or upon the contents of the mind. The aim of each of the different forms of mindfulness is to bring about awareness in all areas of life. The individual is being asked to reach a clear-sighted awareness of himself or herself at all times through observing actions, behaviour, feelings and thoughts. This is by no means easy. In time, however, it brings a sense of detachment, discrimination and self-awareness. The individual is put into the position of being able to see through ploys, tactics and the games that too often enter into emotional relationships. Awareness brings with it the responsibility to change. People are often shocked to discover their own motives, emotional indulgence instead of honest feeling, indulging the personal ego at the expense of others and self-satisfaction rather than self awareness. The very act of discovery starts the balancing process, though it is never easy. We frequently discover things about ourselves that we do not like and this can be difficult for us. We also discover just how deeply we identify with transitory states of feeling. Ouspensky stressed the value of detached observation when he wrote:

> Observe yourself very carefully and you will see that it is not you, but it speaks within you, moves, feels, laughs and cries in you, just as it rains, clears up and rains again outside you. Everything happens in you and your first job is to observe and watch it happening.[13]

The detachment that Ouspensky aimed for is not easily achieved. Yet we can fully appreciate the reasons for it even if we cannot fully experience the quality within ourselves. If we strongly identify with one particular view of ourselves then we will always be vulnerable to its hold over us. Meditation changes the view of the self by altering what we truly identify with. There is a particular meditation which appears in slightly different forms in several traditions. It simply poses the question 'Who am I?' It answers this question by altering the normally held view of the self. The meditation continues, 'I am not my body, I am not my feelings, I am not my thoughts, I am a centre of pure consciousness.' When the individual has truly internalized this idea and made it a living reality then a step has been taken towards personal freedom.

If we look at some of the negative human emotions, we find a long list: jealousy, fear, anger, hatred and many more besides. They each have a different expression but share a common cause, a distorted view of the self. The self that knows its own true nature does not fear, is not angry, jealous or full of hate. Such things tend to fall away like outgrown clothing. The individual discovers new goals which provide inner fulfilment and personal satisfaction. There is no longer any need to compare oneself with others. The new self is liberated from the old imprisoning ideas and attitudes. Positive emotions simply replace negative ones as the individual discovers a new view of self. Meditation is concerned with the expansion of personal awareness. It revolves especially around the question 'Who am I?' The answer is the search itself.

Meditation is a process of stripping away layers of supposed reality, releasing us from the illusions that trap us within a limited world of our own construction. Meditation brings an expanded view of the self and what is ultimately real. Horizons, both personal and impersonal constantly broaden and change. The emotional life is put into context and proper perspective. It is neither denied nor relegated to an inferior place but accorded a part within the balanced whole. As the focus of reality shifts a transcendent view of the larger world comes into view. Personal trials pall into insignificance after meditating on the suffering of the wider group. Meditation on death whether personal or non-personal puts daily life into a different perspective and can be a very salutary experience. Meditation is not about running away from personal feelings but about understanding them, not about vanquishing them but about realizing their validity, not about degrading them but about raising them up to their highest expression. Regular meditation brings profound changes within the emotional life. The individual is better able to cope with the circumstances of daily life, is more in touch with real personal feelings and more able to empathize with the feelings of others. We see this in the image of the Compassionate Buddha who offers an all-embracing love towards all living creatures. Personal love grows into a love which is not limited. Take up meditation for yourself and experience what it has to offer you.

——— Meditation and Mental Well-Being ———

We would all agree that we each possess a mind and that we are each capable of thinking. Indeed we do use it all of the time but to what end? Do we really put our minds to good use? How many of us ever use more than a fraction of our mental capabilities? How many of us are truly creative, able to take an imagined idea and translate it into practical reality? How many of us even retain the faculty of the imagination past childhood? How many of us think clearly at all? How aware are you of your own mental processes? What do you think about and with what results? Can you concentrate easily or does your attention wander? Do you feel that you are allowing your mind to vegetate or are you stimulated by new ideas, projects and interests? Do you feel the need to be able to think more clearly? Do you feel the need to explore your own mental potential?

The mind is a mysterious phenomenon. It has puzzled philosophers and scientists alike for centuries. It is clear that we each possess a mind, yet where does it reside? What is the exact relationship between the mind and the brain? Are they one and the same? We may not be able to point to the mind nor even define it to anyone's satisfaction but we are all aware of its importance to us as thinking people. We each value our own mental well-being. When we are mentally troubled, anxious and strained we feel as if we are living under a cloud. When our minds are clear, we have more mental energy, we enjoy a challenge, we work well and creatively. We are at our most creative and fulfilled when we are free to channel our mental energies into a chosen area. Can meditation help us to achieve a state of mental well-being?

Many people come to meditation in the false belief that it is simple, merely a question of closing one's eyes and drifting away somewhere pleasant. The degree of mental discipline required often comes as quite a surprise. Meditation requires active and sustained concentration upon a particular topic, idea or image. This state of onepointedness enables the mind to become totally absorbed in the object of the meditation which permits realizations to arise within consciousness.

The major meditation systems utilize remarkably similar techniques, particularly in the early stages. Exercises in sheer concentration are universal. Several systems commence mental training with an exercise which consists of watching one's own breath. It is sometimes called 'Mindfulness of Breathing'. It sounds very easy. Anyone who has tried it will know otherwise. The meditator is asked to sit motionless and poised and to become aware of his or her own breathing, not to alter it in any way, merely to become conscious of the natural flow. Another variation of this technique is to count the breaths from one to ten and then begin again. This also sounds deceptively simple. In practice we discover just how difficult it is. We find that our thoughts are distracted, our attention wanders, we are anything but one-pointed. We are brought face to face with our own undisciplined thoughts. Images rush by, the mind starts to deal with a pressing problem, we suddenly remember something we should have done, the list is endless. We realize with a shock just how little control we are able to exert over our own thoughts.

If we persevere with the simple daily routine of watching the breath we gradually find the distractions become fewer and our attention does not wander quite so easily. We begin to understand the meaning of mental concentration. This is the start of meditation proper. This is the start of our own mental training. There is much to be learned as we begin to exert some degree of conscious control over our own thoughts. It is as if we are seeing into the mind for the first time. We discover that our thoughts are normally a stream of disconnected images, memories and ideas. The mind seems to chatter away to itself like a babbling child which will not be quietened. We find that we have been living in a mental jumble. We begin to wonder how we ever achieved anything through the power of our own minds. Gradually we begin to develop the ability to concentrate and to recall the track of our own thoughts.

In time the mental training will spill over into our daily life. We find that we are able to accomplish a difficult mental task more easily. We see a solution to a problem more quickly than we had anticipated. We find that we are absorbing new information quicker than we used to. The response will be personal but there is invariably a sharpening of the mind and its faculties. At this point, when a degree of concentration has been achieved, several systems proceed by introducing the student to the creation of specific types of mental imagery. Certain pictures or images are created within the mind and then reflected upon. This also sounds fairly straightforward. In practice it is quite difficult to hold the concentration for any period of time. Initially the student might be asked to visualize a simple image such as a candle flame or single colour. This sounds like an easy task but as soon as we try to hold one image we also see a host of others. As soon as we begin to reflect upon it, the image fades or is replaced by something entirely different. Again we are brought face to face with our poor ability to concentrate and carry out a simple mental task. With experience and increased powers of concentration and reflection, the student moves on from simple to complex images, often creating entire mental landscapes. The meditator not only constructs the entire moving landscape but also projects into it as an active participant consciously responding to the inner scenes. It bears some relationship to the notion of a consciously produced dream. Some systems also introduce symbolic designs for the purpose of reflection or contemplation. These can be relatively simple or extremely complicated. The meditator projects personal consciousness into the image so that it can be explored from within.

Visual meditations in particular draw upon the faculty of the creative imagination which is latent within each of us. The act of drawing upon the visual imagination in meditation seems to awaken it as a creative force. Once tapped it becomes more active and spontaneously surfaces within the context of daily life. Many people experience bursts of high creativity as they discover new aspects of themselves. It is possible to draw directly upon meditational images as a source of inspiration for creative expression. Such creative expression is not only rewarding but serves outwardly to establish the inner meaning of the personal symbols. The process of meditation can act as a doorway into the latent levels of inner creativity. It seems to unlock aspects of personal expression as part of the exploration into self. Regular meditation brings out creativity in those who would not normally think of themselves as being artistically inclined. It also heightens appreciation of all the creative arts. The inner language of symbols is universal. Personal experience of symbolic forms through meditation opens the doorway to a wider understanding of all symbolic language. The artistic endeavours of mankind whether through art or architecture so often express universal themes. Your own meditational experiences will put you in touch with these great expressions.

The concentration required by meditational discipline will also affect the tasks of daily life. The intensity of meditational absorption can be transferred to any mental task whether it is connected with leisure or work so that mental energy is not wasted and diffused. The ability to apply concentrated mental energy to tasks becomes both natural and effortless. Self-awareness of the scattered and random nature of our normal thought patterns serves as a powerful corrective. We can begin actively to take control of what we think and how we think, putting the power of our own minds to good purpose. With patience we learn to exclude unwanted thoughts and bring the mind back to a central point of attention. It is as if the accumulated cobwebs of the years are cleared away with a resulting increase in clarity and sharpness of thought. Mental confusion and muddled thinking fall away as deeper levels of mental awareness are experienced. Regular meditation keeps the mind active, alert and ever young. When awareness is focused directly on the mind itself we open the door to new possibilities as the mind begins to reveal its true nature. We have been so used to thinking intellectually, that is about things, not sharing a direct experience with them that quite new and deeper perceptions can be quite surprising. Intellectual thought is a useful tool though a limited one. Meditation does not devalue the place of the intellect but balances it with the development of the intuition and the growth of total consciousness which handles all life situations with skilful means. This becomes an all-encompassing perception, far more complete and piercing than sheer intellectualization. When the mind is opened, so wisdom comes to birth and in the fullness of time will make its presence felt. This cannot be explained, only experienced as higher levels of mind come into activity. In daily life meditation brings benefits to all activities and endeavours as each becomes a closer reflection of the true nature. Take up meditation and begin the process for yourself.

Meditation and
Spiritual Well-Being

The spiritual aspect of ourselves is perhaps the most difficult to define or describe in simple terms. We are all aware of the physical, emotional and mental parts of ourselves, but how do we become aware of a spiritual dimension within us? How do we find this part of ourselves, where do we need to look?

The spiritual quest takes many forms but always bears the same hallmark: the incessant search for meaning within life, and the unremitting search for purpose which is grounded within the day-to-day experiences of our own lives. It is not something somehow remote from daily living but it is rather the groundplan of it. We often make a conscious attempt to establish our own spiritual values by first mixing with people of various spiritual and religious persuasions as we attempt to understand their guiding principles and beliefs. We may even move from one group to another taking a little knowledge here, a little comfort there, until we finally discover a spiritual framework that suits us. People invariably know when they have 'come home' for something within them seems to resonate comfortably. Most who consciously search discover a spiritual environment in which they can grow. This process is something we can each identify with. Essentially our quest is the search for meaning, the search for the self and ultimately the search for reality. What has meditation to offer the seeker?

Unlike the major organized religions, meditation lays down no dogma or creed. It does not ask you to accept a body of teaching. Instead you are actively required to take up the search for yourself through the meditation exercises. You are asked to look into yourself in a particular way and to make your own discoveries. You learn through your own realizations. You are at the hub of the system. The onus is upon you to maintain practice and be self-disciplined. You cannot place the responsibility for your spiritual life upon someone else. It is given squarely into your hands from the outset. Meditation is no easy option. It is worth remembering again that each of the major meditation systems developed within the highly disciplined and rigid framework of withdrawn monastic life. It is a mistake to see it as a liberal and easy-going approach to the spiritual life. We would do well to recall the rigours of the withdrawn and dedicated life even if we are not subject to the same discipline.

Meditation begs that you search out your own inner nature: it does not present you with ready-made answers. It leads you towards your own understanding through personal experience. It systematically exposes you to all the illusions which create a false sense of identity. In this way it brings about personal realizations of what is ultimately real. Meditation commences by working directly upon the self. Yet at the same time this opens up the search for the Absolute, the Void, the Divine which is intimately related to the search for the self. It is a commonly held conception that man is the mirror-image of Divinity. Man is the microcosm, the lesser world. Divinity is the macrocosm, the greater world. There exists a direct relationship between the two. If you would know the one, look to the other. We cannot know God but we can know ourselves.

Meditation does not produce idiosyncratic and purely personal responses. On the contrary, meditation seems to elicit universal responses which are personally experienced. Students working within a given system frequently experience similiar realizations as they progress through the various levels of the work. The emphasis is always upon personal experience and realization. How else do we ever truly understand?

Meditation is also a quest for knowledge. It is knowledge which belongs to a higher order. It is neither the amassing of facts nor the application of data, but simply *knowing* in itself. The Tibetan term for this is *sherab,* wisdom. It means ultimate, primary or higher knowledge. We find the idea of higher knowledge throughout all sacred writings. The term *tantra,* which referred to an ancient and complete system for self-unfoldment, means 'the knowledge that saves'. The term *upanishad'* (the *Upanishads* are a part of the Hindu scriptures), means 'knowledge which liberates from bondage'. Here we have significant clues as to the nature of what we shall discover. It is knowledge which will change us and bring freedom.

What kind of knowledge does meditation bring? Meditation brings self-knowledge and ultimately knowledge of what is real and what is only transient. This distinction between different levels of reality, some being less 'real', and others being more 'real' is an extraordinary concept only shared by mystics and physicists. Neither accept the appearance of reality at face value. The ultimate quest for transcendence might not seem to concern the vast majority of individuals who take up meditation. It is too obscure and distant a goal, even too tortuous a path. Yet for some this remains the beckoning light no matter what. In Zen it is said that the desire for enlightenment should be total and passionate. The man who falls into a deep pit thinks of nothing but how to get out, so the individual who seeks enlightenment puts all available energy into the goal. Such passion and commitment is rarely seen. Each major meditation system has its own way to the intrinsic goal. The system of Kundalini Yoga seeks to raise consciousness to a cosmic level through the active arousal of the inner powers and the final opening of the crown *chakra* (energy centre), the thousand petalled lotus. Zen seeks Enlightenment, *satori*, in deliverance from all the illusions that entrap. In Hinduism the ultimate quest is for *moksha,* release. To a Sufi the ulitmate state is *baqa.* The Christian equivalent is the Kingdom of Heaven.

Few of us really feel ready or able to reach out to these exalted states. We find it difficult to imagine what such states might mean in terms of human experience. Our minds cannot grasp the actual reality of such an experience unless of course we too have shared a glimpse of a transcendent level of reality. The nearest we can come to understanding the quality of such an experience is perhaps through metaphor. The modern Zen teacher Philip Kapleau reminds us of the state of satori with reference to a wristwatch. The face represents our own life, time, space, birth and death, cause and effect. The reverse side represents the changeless undifferentiated aspect of life. We normally see only the front of the watch; but should we suddenly be able to flip it over for the first time seeing the connection between the face and the back, the relative and the absolute, we have touched satori, enlightenment. We may struggle with such images – that is their purpose. We may read with profit the accounts of those who have partaken in such experiences. They are often called mystics. Mystical experiences have been recorded throughout history. They cut across the normal cultural and religious boundaries. Such experiences are remarkably similar in form and content. There is a directness and intensity in such accounts that is both convincing and thought-provoking. The Indian poet Rabindranath Tagore had a mystical experience while watching a sunrise. It made such an impression on him that he wrote about it to a friend:

As I was watching it suddenly in a moment, a veil seemed to be lifted from my eye. I found the world wrapped in an

inexpressible glory with its waves of joy and beauty bursting
and breaking on all sides. The thick cloud of sorrow that lay
on my heart in many folds was pierced through by the light of
the world, which was everywhere radiant. ... There was no-
one whom I did not love at that moment.[14]

This experience is typical of its kind. Tagore suddenly and without
warning felt he was able to see beyond the confines of normal
reality and what he witnessed was glorious and beyond
description. It filled him with great love. Such moments, though
often brief, seem to convey a sense of reality which outweighs all
other experiences. Dr Richard Maurice Bucke had a sudden and
illuminating experience at the age of thirty-six which so impressed
him that he went on to collect and investigate other such
experiences. He recorded his own experience which radically
altered the course of his life:

I had spent an evening in a great city, with two friends. I was
in a state of quiet even passive enjoyment, not actually
thinking but letting ideas, images and emotions flow of
themselves as it were. All at once, without warning of any
kind, I found myself wrapped in a flame coloured cloud. For
an instant I thought of fire, an immense conflagration
somewhere close by in that great city. The next instant I knew
that the fire was myself. Directly afterwards there came upon
me a sense of exultation of immense joyousness,
accompanied by or immediately followed by an intellectual
illumination quite impossible to describe. Among other
things, I did not merely come to believe, I saw that the
universe is not composed of dead matter, but is on the
contrary, a living Presence. I became conscious myself of
eternal life. It was not a conviction that I would have eternal
life, but a consciousness that I possessed eternal life. Then I
saw that all men are immortal, that the cosmic order is such
that without any peradventure all things work together for
the good of each and all, that the foundation principle of the
world, of all the worlds is what we call love and the
happiness of each and all is in the long run certain. The vision
lasted but a few seconds and was gone, but the memory of it
and the sense of reality of it has remained.[15]

Such experiences are not as rare as might be expected. In varying
degrees moments of illumination and profound insight have been

experienced by many people. This transcendent state of awareness seems to break through quite unbidden on occasion. Often it does not last and is never repeated. It is but a brief glimpse of something that we cannot hold onto. When the ground of consciousness has been tilled through the techniques of spiritual discipline it becomes possible to enter this state at will and in full consciousness; this is satori, moksha, baqa, liberation. It is the goal of the journey and perhaps the starting place for another. It is a goal rarely achieved yet the fact that some have attained this state makes it accessible even if only at a distant level of perception for all of us. We can be certain that the mystical experience is real even though we are at a loss to explain it. Even those who have experienced such transcendent states of awareness find it difficult to describe the experience in language that makes it comprehensible to others. Words seem woefully inadequate to convey the totality of an experience which is so far outside the realms of everyday life. From the accounts that we have, we can, however, say that the mystical state is characterized by certain elements. Many things seem to happen instantaneously so that the moment no matter how brief carries great weight and importance. Knowledge is conveyed in a sudden flash through insight without any formal reasoning. The normal thought processes are momentarily transcended. There is a sense of timelessness, a sense only of the eternal present. The individual feels as if he or she has entered into the Oneness of Life and briefly experienced the harmony of all things. Suddenly the cosmic dimension of reality is revealed. Against the vast and eternal backdrop the personality appears transient yet the eternal dimension of existence is also experienced so that another level of personal being is perceived. So powerful is this kind of experience that it can totally transform the individual. Blaise Pascal, the mystic and mathematician, underwent a mystical experience which so marked him that his account of it was stitched into his clothing and discovered upon his death:

In the year of grace 1654 ...
From about half past ten in the evening to
about half an hour after midnight.
FIRE
God of Abraham, God of Isaac, God of Jacob,
Not the God of philosophers and scholars.
Absolute certainty: Beyond reason. Joy. Peace.

Forgetfulness of the world and everything but God.
The world has not known thee, but I have known thee.
Joy! Joy! Joy! Tears of Joy.[16]

The mystical state more than any other defies explanation and rationalization but remains perfectly real nonetheless. It seems that in such moments we come face to face with a level of reality which is normally hidden from us. The mystical experience remains a mystery yet it points the way to unseen dimensions and states of being. Through the eyes of the mystics we can glimpse a greater reality, through their hearts we can feel the surge of universal love and through their vision we can expand our own. Meditation is the key, the portal and the path by which we may travel and discover spiritual well-being for ourselves.

CHAPTER 3

THE TECHNIQUES OF MEDITATION

At first sight the many and varied techniques of meditation may appear confusing or even contradictory. What does a chanting group meditation have in common with a solitary Buddhist monk mindfully counting his own breath? What does the conundrum-like koan have in common with the complex and highly visual meditation of a Tibetan monk? They may indeed be quite different in technique and form yet the underlying discipline, intention and goals are very similar. It is always to this unity in diversity that we should look rather than be diverted by surface differences. In fact when an individual has been trained in one system there should be no difficulty in experiencing the meditation forms of another.

Meditations can be separated into different types for the purpose of clarity. This division suits our purposes. We will look first at the types of meditation that employ a form on inner image making.

Visual Meditations

Visual meditations employ the natural facility of the mind to create images, that is to see with the mind's eye. Theoretically there is nothing that cannot be reproduced from memory or from the imagination. This faculty is innate though it can also be improved with particular forms of practice. In the early stages of meditation experience the individual may simply fix the gaze upon an object such as a candle flame. The *Visuddhimagga*, the fifth-century Buddhist text, may be thought of in modern terms as a map for inner exploration.[17] It lists a series of objects or *kasinas* which can be used as meditation devices. Ten separate devices are used. They are the four elements of earth, air, fire and water, the four colours blue, yellow, red and white, with the addition of light and space. The student is directed to utilize the physical counterpart of the element where appropriate; a bowl of water, a flame, a dish of earth and the action of the wind are each suggested. When meditating on the four colours it is suggested that a disc of the appropriate colour is used. It is also suggested that the student uses physical items of the appropriate colour such as blue paint, blue flowers, blue cloth, yellow paper, yellow straw, red flowers, white pebbles and white snow. Meditation on light is focused on subjects such as light through a window, light through foliage, sunlight and moonlight. Meditation on space is focused on spaces between objects, spaces between buildings, a sky and an empty bowl for example. The subjects suggested remain as pertinent today as when they were first written down. The modern student might safely borrow them as initial encounters in visual meditation.

Having a physical object on which to focus the mind helps to keep the concentration centred and serves to establish the understanding that ultimately meditation concerns our relationship to the world about us. In practice the student might prepare a particular focus point and sit before it for a while absorbing its details. Then the eyes are closed and the image is then reproduced within the mind. The image itself is then meditated upon and contemplated in every way possible. Initially we tend to think about the object. For instance if we were to take the element of water as a meditation point, we would probably find ourselves thinking about the uses and functions of water and we would draw on memories to provide personal experiences. At this stage we are still thinking *about* water and have not yet really entered into rapport with the subject. However, if we should sink into the subject and become one with it we might experience the feeling of flow, or the pull of the moon, the sensation of movement or the power of the flood. This is quite a different matter and will create an entirely new understanding of water. The individual progresses from visualizing simple objects to more complicated constructions. With experience, entire landscapes and moving scenes can be meditated upon. This only comes after considerable practice with creating and sustaining mental forms.

The aim of this particular form of meditation is not the creation of images in themselves but the response that such images evoke from the individual. The creation of the image is only the means to an end, not the end in itself. This is sometimes confused especially in the beginning when the individual can become wrapt by this newly discovered inner artistry. Once the technique has been acquired it is immensely rewarding as there are no limitations to the focus points for meditation which can become increasingly more abstract yet still rendered tangible through the creative imagination. The technique requires not merely the creation of moving mental pictures but absorption into them so that consciousness is projected into the single image, the symbolic form or even the more complex scenario. In this way the individual is able to explore the image from within as opposed to simply observing it from the outside. Even a very simple object such as a flower has a lot to teach. We might find ourselves discovering its qualities, essence and life force. A great deal can be learned this way about the many things that we take for granted. Gradually consciousness expands beyond the limited personal realm to embrace the living forms of nature, the cyclic movements of change, the ebb and flow of life itself.

The altered awareness of the meditation state is quite unlike the rational and deductive thinking that we normally use to inform us about the world. We learn something directly from the experience. We are informed by our own senses, which become attuned to the world about us. We are beginning to work directly with our own level of awarenss. As proficiency comes we can create complex inner scenes for personal meditation. The Christian for example might choose to meditate upon the life of Christ by inwardly creating and experiencing particular scenes as in the exercises set by St Ignatius Loyola. This is rather like creating an internal passion play. There is much to be learned from this. In Tibetan meditation we find the art of visualization at its most complex. Inner images of immense detail are created in the mind. The student will be asked to create living pictures of the gods with specific and complex details. In Tibetan meditation it is common practice to use images of various gods and goddesses to personify living universal forces. The student identifies totally with the particular god-form and comes to understand and embody the quality so represented. To the initiate trained in the system each detail of colour, dress, gesture or stance for example will convey particular symbolic meanings. The image as a whole summarizes a vast range of knowledge and application. The workings of vast cosmic laws and the dynamic interrelationship between various forces can all be presented to the student in a form that will evoke personal devotional response and realization. The following example shows something of the complexity and detail involved in the creation of just one image. It is described by Chogym Trungpa:

> On the disc of the autumn moon, clear and pure you place a
> seed syllable. The rays of the seed syllable emanate immense
> cooling compassion that radiates beyond the limits of sky or
> space. It fulfills the needs and desires of sentient beings
> bringing warmth so that confusions may be clarified. Then
> from the seed syllable you create a Mahavairocana Buddha,
> white in colour, with the features of an aristocrat – an eight
> year old child with a beautiful, innocent, pure, powerful,
> royal gaze. He is dressed in the costume of a medieval king of
> India. He wears a glittering gold crown inlaid with
> wishfulfilling jewels. Part of his long black hair floats over his
> shoulders and back; the rest is made into a topknot
> surmounted by a glittering blue diamond. He is seated cross
> legged on the lunar disc with his hands in the meditation
> mudra holding a vajra (sceptre) carved from pure white
> crystal.[18]

Here is a complex symbolic picture which can directly inform the
individual who is in possession of the inner keys. Without such
keys it remains only an image. With them it becomes a living
vehicle of spiritual reality.

It is not only in the East that symbolic visualization is used as a
means of conveying intuitive truth and inner reality. The traditional
Western form of meditation also has its own system of image-
making. This tradition owes much to the figure of the storyteller
bard or wandering poet. In the distant past such a figure might
have travelled from settlement to settlement with a store of
traditional tales. The storyteller was far more than a mere reciter of
tales. His apprenticeship was long and arduous demanding a
lifetime of study. He would have been the living heir to a long
tradition of oral knowledge, a repository of wisdom passed down
by his forebears. His storytelling combined the heroic with the
supersensory, the past and the future, the living and the dead. He
was wise-man, shaman, priest, poet, recorder of deeds and
initiator. When the meal had been taken and the wine drunk, and
the fires were aglow, he would begin to weave his tales of
otherwordly places, of gods and heroes, of questing adventures
and personal peril. As he spoke, the listeners would participate by
building the inner landscapes, each travelling the journey within
their own minds. In such a simple and natural setting, creative

listening became an act of creative imagination and the meditative art was born.

It is difficult for those not experienced in the techniques of the creative imagination to comprehend the power of the mind to generate images, not as make-believe nor as intellectual pretence but as a way into another dimension, as a means of bringing forth the numinous. Today we have largely given up this inner process in favour of television, cinema and the vast array of other visual imagery that surrounds us. We need to retrain this latent ability through exercise, concentration, and meditation so that it becomes second nature again.

The use of god-forms as a means of expressing universal forces is an ancient and widespread tradition. We find it in both the Eastern and Western systems. A particular image will personify a universal quality and serve as a vehicle for it. At its simplest it might be thought of as a form of mental shorthand. Who can think of Venus without thinking of love? Each tradition has developed its own images and symbols. They serve to embody the spiritual realizations of the group and to preserve them in accessible form. Heroic and mythic tales serve to keep the spiritual wisdom of the race alive.

Traditional mythology is always a rich source for meditation. It is within mythology that we encounter universal powers most easily. It is the forging of our relationship with these fundamental patterns which helps us to relate to the greater cycles about us. Jung outlined a number of recurring images. Of these a group of seven are especially significant. These are the archetypes of the Feminine, the Masculine, the Self, the Hero, the Adversary, Death–Rebirth, and the Quest. These severn patterns alone give a deep insight into mythology, religious beliefs and spiritual systems. We will find them in various guises in every major tradition. It is curious how often these same themes occur in various mythologies. We can trace the patterns in the legend of Isis and Osiris, in the Babylonian or Greek tales. We will always discover the same motifs operating no matter where we look. These archetypal patterns are changeless and universal. We are as much influenced by them as our forbears and distant ancestors. If we look clearly we can still see these patterns appearing within our own lives. Certain forms of meditation actively incorporate archetypal material as a means of integrating various aspects of the psyche. These meditations tend to be charged and highly transformative in their effect. Such symbols react directly with the psyche and invariably create a powerful response.

Meditation is a powerful tool for personal change. It works directly upon all the aspects of being. Therefore meditation should be a graded activity commencing with basic exercises which later become more inwardly demanding. We find that traditional systems acknowledge the need for graded material by following a very particular structure. In Buddhism, the path of Jhana precedes that of Vipassana, that is to say the development of concentration precedes the expansion of insight. Where the approach of mindulness is used, it begins first with the breath before proceeding to other aspects. The notion of a meditational structure ensures that tasks keep pace with the gradually changing and expanding experiences of the individual. This structure is easily preserved within traditionally organized environments such as the ashram where everything proceeds according to traditional precedence. It is also preserved in the systems of Tibet and India where the pupil–teacher relationship is still followed with great care. We in the West have neither and are perhaps in danger of losing sight of the value of a structured system. Do-It Yourself may be ideal for home maintenance, it is not always perfect for maintenance of the self.

Mandalas and Yantras

Visualization can be used to create images and pictures entirely from the imagination. It can also be used for the internal exploration of a pre-established *mandala* image. Mandala simply means 'circle'. This form so naturally and obviously represents the flow of life that it appears universally in spiritual and religious settings. Jung became interested in this form when such images began to arise spontaneously in his dream life. He began to paint and preserve them, like any other student discovering inner spiritual dimensions. He even wrote about them in his autobiography, so important were they in his growing awareness. He realized that the emerging mandalas were images of the totality of the self. It brought him to the realization that the self is actively at work as a reflection of the Monad, the One, Unity. He had come to see the reality of the correspondence between the microcosm and the macrocosm expressed by the Hermetic philosophers in the form 'As above so below'.

The form of the circle naturally lends itself to the portrayal of the symbolic life force both personal and transpersonal. It is a living symbol. We see the circular form as an integral part of dance, especially where this is used to express group – rather than individual – aspirations. We can place all the turning point of our lives upon the circle. We can see the cycle of the seasons and the less tangible cycles of greater dimensions. The centre point always has a special significance, for it symbolizes both the self and the divine impulse, which can be seen as one and the same. Indeed it is a commonly held metaphysical concept that the Divine Source is the macrocosmic world, while man is the microcosmic world. We find this idea in Sufism, Qabalah and Hinduism. We find it too in Christianity, where it is stated that God created man in his own image.

It is no suprise that we find the mandala appearing wherever man has attempted to express a relationship with the Divine. We see it in the sand paintings of the Navaho, in the sacred dance of the Whirling Dervish, in the Gothic Rose windows and in a great many other places and expressions. But to see the mandala only as a form of sacred art is to miss its truly vital aspect. It is a living sacred form. We discover this most forcibly in the traditions of those who still live within the circular form. Among nomadic dwellers the circular image exerts a powerful harmonizing influence. To the Mongol people, the *yurt*, the tent which is their home, is a sacred reflection of the universal patterns. It is a living mandala which forms the groundplan of their daily living in the most literal sense. (See figure 2.) The hearth burns at the centre, the sacred point. Everything has its appointed place within the yurt to reflect the order of the universe.

The mandala appears widely as a religious symbol. The form is universal; the contents are particular to the culture. Some mandalas are extremely complex, others are very simple; the principle remains the same in either case. The mandala expresses universal truths in symbolic form which the student may come to understand through meditation. Tibetan Buddhism has perhaps taken the mandala to its fullest expression, certainly to its most complex. Here we find extremely beautiful and intricate cosmograms which are works of art in their own right. These depict universal laws as personified by deities and demons. They are part of the life of the monastery and are passed down through the generations. Others are simply traced out in the earth with

The Yurt and the Universe — a Mandala

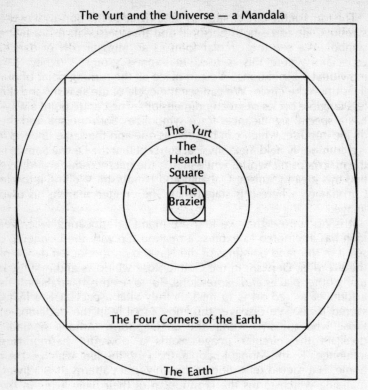

Figure 2

powders of different colours and ornamented with sticks of incense or representations of particular deities in dough. These temporary mandalas often serve as teaching aids in the interaction between teacher and pupil. The pupil works with the mandala images by identifying himself with their essence, absorbing their dynamic qualities and thereby transforms the level of personal consciousness. It is here that we frequently come across the use of various god-forms as personifications of divine forces. Such images are invariably highly complex as they are designed to open the mind up to the dynamic interplay of cosmic powers which are personified as deities. The now famous Tibetan mandala, the Wheel of Life depicts the workings of the cosmos at many levels. The meditator internally visualizes the complex imagery and then goes on to project his own consciousness into the various aspects of the mandala, taking on the living energies of the universal forces contained within it. This requires a steady concentration and a highly developed visual imagination which comes only after much training and refinement.

It is a mistake to think that the mandala belongs exclusively to the East. The West has its own mandalas in the form of Christian and even pre-Christian symbols. Our traditional heritage of spiritual images has been much impoverished by the biblical injunction not to worship any graven image. This prohibition has been used at various times to wage war on symbolic and representational forms. It has given rise to misunderstanding and even persecution. The mandala is not an image for worship. It is a focus for meditation. It can be very revealing to allow your own images to emerge spontaneously and become the foundation for a personal mandala.

The close cousin of the mandala is the *yantra*. This is a purely geometric design often set within a circle. The yantra combines triangles, circles and squares in patterns of cosmic significance. In common with the mandala the centre point has a special significance which is very often pinpointed by a dot, the *bindu* point. The meditation will often begin and end at this axial point. At the simplest level the circle stands for the Absolute. The interlaced triangles represent the mystical union of heavenly and earthly forces. The square represents the forces of manifestation.

The idea that geometric forms symbolize certain universal laws is a very old one. It found favour with both Pythagoras and Plato. Indeed mathematics can be seen as an expression of the inner laws of the universe. The yantra might be thought of as a mathematical equation or even the formula of a scientist. To the initiate trained in its use, the yantra offers a formula in applied spiritual science. It brings the individual into contact with certain transpersonal qualities through private meditation and inner exploration.

There are many traditional yantras. Most are not widely known, though there is perhaps one exception, which is the Tantric Buddhist one shown in figure 3. It has come to prominence in the West mainly through the cultural interchange of the sixties. It is a particularly significant yantra as it expresses the energies of the *mantra Aum* (mantras are discussed below, after the next paragraph). It is commonly believed that each yantra is the literal embodiment of the cosmic forces that it describes. This makes the

Figure 3

yantra a particularly powerful form of meditation. In figure 4 we see a Kali yantra. It is designed to activate the Kali forces within the psyche of the devotee. Without the inner keys it remains only an image. To the initiate of Kali it is the door to a particular series of experiences.

The Eastern mandala and yantra serve the same function as the Western descriptive meditation even though they differ in form. The forces which are represented within the mandala are also experienced within the form of the inner journey. Both systems portray the same forces, merely under a different guise. There are a variety of meditations which use the technique of visualization in

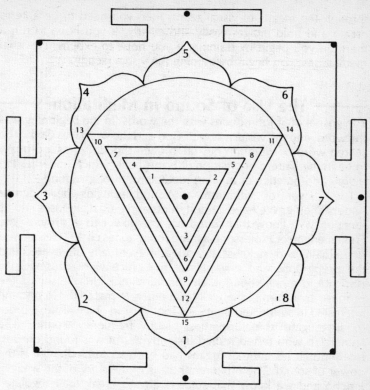

Figure 4   Āvarana (surrounding) deities invoked in the Kālī Yantra. In the 15 angles of the triangle: 1 Kālī, 2 Kapālinī, 3 Kulla, 4 Kurukulla, 5 Virodhinī, 6 Vipracittā, 7 Ugrā, 8 Ugraprabhā, 9 Diptā, 10 Nīlā, 11 Chanā, 12 Balākā, 13 Mātrā, 14 Mudrā, 15 Mitā. In the 8 lotus petals: 1 Brahmī; 2 Indrānī; 3 Māhesvarī; 4 Cāmundā; 5 Kaumārī; 6 Aprājitā; 7 Vārāhī; 8 Nārsimhī; and the traditional deities of the eight regents of space. After the tantric work Kālī Tantra

one way or another. The use of visualization as a meditational tool requires that the creative imagination be suitably developed and refined. This only comes with practice. Sometimes the initial training period is felt to be rather tedious and unexciting, but it is a necessary preparatory stage. If you hope to experience meditation through the means of visualization then you need to be able to create and hold images easily and clearly. If you hope to run a marthon you begin by training. If you hope to experience visual meditations, you begin by training the visual faculty.

—— The Use of Sound in Meditation——

The gospel of St John opens with the words 'In the beginning was the word, and the word was with God and the word was God'. The sacred word or vibration has often been thought of as a primary force in the pattern of creation. It is this belief which underlies the theory and practice of *mantra*; meditation through sound.

The power of vibration as sound remains beyond our understanding. We have, at best, hints and partial glimpses into its function. We know that sound has the power to destroy, as the French engineer Professor Gavraud found to his cost.[19] He suffered perpetually from sickness at work and eventually discovered that the proportions and materials of the office were causing it to resonate to a neighbouring air-conditioning plant. He solved the problem by covering the walls in a different material. He became interested in sound and built a six-foot version of a whistle in order to investigate the properties of low-frequency sound. The technician who tested it died instantly and it was found on post mortem that his internal organs had been scrambled! Such is the power of sound. The Bible reminds us of the story of the walls of Jericho and we know that soldiers always break their regulated step to cross a bridge. Sound, resonance and vibration are intimately connected; we cannot have one without the other. If sound has the power to destroy might it not also have to power to create and establish order and pattern at some subtle level?

The ancient science of mantra affirms the belief in the positive use of sound both microcosmically and macrocosmically, that is to say personally and at a transcendent level. It has given rise to the practice of group and solitary chanting and intoning. Mantra is the science of sound. Many traditions have grown up concerning the power immanent in the correct pronunciation of a mantra – and the word *must* be sounded correctly for a balanced effect. The subtle understanding required to experience this form of meditation fully can really only be learned at the hands of a teacher. It can be read about but not truly experienced without trained guidance.

Perhaps the most famous mantra of all is Aum. The Hindus take this to be the most sacred of all sounds. This simple sound enshrines an entire philosophy. The three letters are called the three quarters. Each is allotted to one of the three gods of the Hindu trinity. The A is given to Brahman, the Creator. The U is given to Vishnu, the Preserver. Finally the M is allocated to Shiva the Destroyer. When sounded the three different aspects are vibrated as one unified form. The mantra expresses the subtle reality of the Trinity as Three in One and One in Three. The final quarter appears only when the word is sounded and the final M is prolonged and hangs in the air. It is the hidden quarter. It is the response within matter, the consequence within the cause–effect relationship. Sounding the word with this understanding can be very illuminating.

The three letters also refer to three states of being which according to Hindu philosophy, the soul can experience. The first is the state of daily consciousness when the soul sees only the physically manifested universe but has no comprehension of the laws behind it. It is called *Vaisavanara* and is attributed to the letter A. The second state is that of dreaming sleep represented by the U. Here the dreamer creates personal reality and participates in it. There is a growing awareness of the subtle universal forces. This state is called *Taijasa*. The third state is that of dreamless sleep in which the causal world is discovered and realized. It is called *Prajna*. The hidden and final quarter represents the pure consciousness when self-realization is a reality.

Within this single mantra we find an entire philosophy. Here we are reminded of the three stages by which a soul comes to know itself. We remember the three levels of being – gross, subtle and causal. We recall the three aspects of Creation – the emerging, the sustaining and the disintegrating. Here the macrocosmic and microcosmic forces are brought together into one focus point, a single word. A second well-known mantra is *Om Mane Padme Hum*. It is of Tibetan origin and part of a long heritage of sounded words. It is rich in inner symbolism and meaning. True mantra is never just a sound alone. The mantra 'Om Mane Padme Hum' means 'Hail to the radiant jewel in the lotus'. It commences with the sacred syllable which is deep with meaning. The jewel in the lotus is the jewel of self-realization, shining and radiant. It is the hidden jewel of the self awaiting discovery as full consciousness dawns. The lotus is an Eastern symbol for the awakening self. It is worth using this image as a focus for meditation. Its roots lie deeply buried in mud; its stem rises up through the water until the flower opens upon the water in the bright light of day. It focuses the mind on the aspiration to full awakening. It refers to the flowering of the crown chakra, the thousand-petalled lotus at the crown of the head. When this chakra is fully opened, self-realization is born and the jewel shines forth.

The sounding of a mantra is not merely a matter of the creation of sheer physical sound. It is a complete meditation, rich in symbolism and replete with meaning. Yet its form is ultimately simple. Its powerful resonance creates subtle changes and brings total involvement. It is said that a mantra has the power to awaken the dormant forces of the soul as it breaks out of its narrow intellectual confines and sets up inner resonances. Such a thing hardly seems possible to the rational mind.

There are many mantras, from single words to complete phrases. For example a particular seed mantra is attributed to each of the chakras. These centres of force have a physical counterpart which is used as a focus point for meditation. The seed mantras for the chakras are as follows:

> The Base centre, Lam.
> The Pelvic centre, Vam.
> The Navel centre, Ram.
> The Heart centre, Yam.
> The Throat centre, Ham.
> The Brow centre, Om.

These are sounded as a means of awakening the forces of each centre. Each mantra is also connected to certain symbolic ideas. The mantra therefore acts in part as a form of shorthand bringing to mind many other associations. The mantric sound serves as a vehicle for meaning. It has been suggested by some Western writers on meditation that the repitition of *any* sound will suffice. This is untrue. Repitition of a randomly chosen word or phrase may soothe the mind, but it will not produce the profound effects of a genuine mantra. The meaningless mantra is not in accord with ancient teachings. Like a seed, the mantra is rich with potential. It bears symbolic ideas which take root in the mind as the meditator and the mantra become attuned. Sounding a mantra is an active affirmation of spiritual aspiration. The individual participates wholeheartedly in the experience and becomes immersed in the sound and vibration.

Group chanting is a widespread practice. We find it in Buddhism, Hinduism, Sufism and in Judaic practice. Chanting forms a large part of the devotional and ceremonial sessions. In Zen Buddhism group chanting is a daily practice. The group assembles at dawn to the sound of a large standing drum. The drum ceases and instead the sound of a gong resounds to introduce the different chants. A third instrument, another drum, sets a cadence that can be followed by the group. A lead chanter introduces the chants and a chorus of voices respond. Each chanter takes his or her own lowest natural pitch while at the same time blending in with the whole. The sound comes from deep within the belly, the *hara* centre. The words are not sung but vibrated each upon a personal note. It is performed without ego, without conscious effort but in total consciousness. The ensuing experience is total, a sea of sound filled with waves of resonance. There is great energy which belongs to no one but is shared by all.

In Sufism the sounded word is of paramount importance. The central practice is Dhikr, the remembrance of God through repetition of the Holy Names. The most important Sufi mantra is *la ilaha illa Llah*, there is no God but Allah. Here is the foundation of Sufi philosophy in a single phrase. True mantra always has the ability to capture the essential inner quality of an entire philosophy. This Sufi mantra can be equated to the Hindu mantra 'Aum' which also summarizes a spiritual philosophy.

The West also has a tradition of the sounded word though it is perhaps less well-known than its Eastern counterpart. In the teachings of the Qabalah we find a compilation of the Names of God which are used as mantras. This is similar to the Sufi tradition. To sound a Holy Name of God is to aspire to understand its reality and to draw upon the divine qualities thereby effecting a transformation within consciousness. The Christian Church also has, what is in effect a mantra, the Jesus Prayer. The Prayer 'Lord Jesus Christ, Son of God, have mercy on me, a sinner' is intended to be used continuously. It is not a petitionary prayer but a statement of Christian faith. It encapsulates the essence of Christian teaching. In the Greek 'Kyrie eleison', we have a Christian mantra which can be repeated as a meditative spiritual statement.

Seed Thoughts as Meditation

We are all familiar with the process of planting seeds. We take the seed and plant it in good soil. We make sure that it has light and water and then we have the pleasure of watching it unfold. A seed thought is little different. We take a seed, be it a phrase or a fragment of text and plant it within the mind. It is nourished by our continued attendance upon it until finally it takes root within the mind and becomes an established part of consciousness.

Meditation of this kind is found universally. The subject matter is usually a suitable fragment from traditional texts. It might be the words of a teacher or a fundamental concept from within the tradition. A verse of mystical poetry or a phrase which expresses a spiritual truth in a memorable way is also suitable. There is really no limit to relevant material. The entire spiritual heritage of humanity awaits us.

The way to approach this form of experience is to enter the meditational state and keep the seed thought as the constant focus. In the beginning an internal dialogue seems to take place as the mind seeks to establish the parameters of the particular phrase. This stage seems to be inevitable as the mind always seems to choose analysis before synthesis. When the intellectual phase is finally exhausted the mind is then able to move on to more direct insight. The questioning ceases and is replaced by a process of identification. There is a sudden and most definite realization. Finally there comes understanding when the seed thought has blossomed and is integrated into total consciousness.

This sounds quite straightforward – merely thinking about something in depth. In practice the mind tends to wander very easily as there is nothing concrete like a mantra or an image on which to focus. It is also too easy to get bogged down in intellectual discussion in the attempt to reach some definitive answer which is not the object of the exercise. Phrases and sayings are very often chosen because they will not yield to rational thought. Instead the student is asked to dwell upon the language of the mystic or the paradox of spiritual truth.

Suitable material can be found in every spiritual tradition from the Bible to the Koran, from the Hindu scriptures to Hermetic gems. Each tradition has its own treasures to offer. You may stay within your own discipline or gently explore the fabric of another system. Taking a phrase for a seed thought is perhaps the gentlest and safest form of meditation. It is possible to arrange a personal programme of study incorporating phrases for reflection. The possibilities are endless. These suggestions might prove helpful, the Buddhist phrase 'Form is Emptiness, Emptiness is Form', the

Hermetic phrase 'As Above, so Below' or the key phrase 'Man Know Thyself'. The choice is yours.

The Koan

No survey of meditational techniques would be complete without the inclusion of the *koan*, a conundrum which throws a well-aimed spanner into the normal thought processes. It developed out of an earlier practice of rapid question and answer between master and pupil, a form of verbal sparring designed to help the pupil break out of the fetters of conditioned thinking. Originally this encounter took place directly between master and pupil; later on it gave rise to the formalized koan.

Each koan is selected by the teacher to suit the individual temperament and strength of the pupil. To work with a koan requires both concentration and a keen aspiration which only the teacher can assess. A koan is like a riddle, a puzzle without any apparent answer. It is not designed to be answered in the usual understanding of the word but to arouse the 'doubt mass'. This burning perplexity becomes focused and provides a driving intensity with which to tackle the koan. The student may be assigned a koan which will last several months. It is to be worked on unremittingly day and night so that every energy is applied to it. The koan is not worked on in an intellectual manner. It has to become a total part of the student's thinking. It is first recited in the mind, as if in slow motion. Each syllable is dwelt upon and synchronized with the flow of breath so that the koan enters the body as well as the mind. This creates a state of total concentration, *samadhi*. In this state of deep concentration the focus of attention is maintained constantly. There is an internal tension which builds up as the resolution is sought. Even in the middle of winter a student can be seen to be wet with beads of perspiration as the internal struggle goes on. Eventually a realization will come, the resolution is discovered.

The koan works by 'breaking asunder the mind of ignorance and opening the eye of truth'. It is designed to precipitate awakening by breaking through the limited confines of consciousness. In Zen, enlightenment is said to happen when a breakthrough takes place on all levels of consciousness at once. Directed energy focused through the koan may be sufficient to do this. This particular technique cannot be experienced outside the teacher–pupil relationship in Zen training itself. To work with a koan involves great inner stuggle. There is always the fear that it will never show its solution, that the riddle will remain. Yet there are solutions to be experienced and with the teacher's help the student invariably reaches a point of realization.

The first koan to be recorded is that which a great Zen Master, Hui-Neng, posed when beset by robbers. He persuaded them to sit in silence. He then asked them 'When you are thinking of neither good nor evil, what is at that moment your original face?' Thus was the first koan born and the style set for questions without answers. Some koans have become well-known. Others are told in the form of stories. Each has a curious fascination and leaves the mind slightly numbed at first. What is the sound of one hand clapping? Has the dog a Buddha Nature? What was your original face before your parents were born? These are but some of the more well-known koans. The most inscrutable, however, must surely be the koan 'Mu'. One is simply lost for words, which is the object of the exercise.

Solving a koan is a process which requires the supervision of a teacher if it is to fulfil its purpose. There is a delicate balance between pushing the mind beyond the intellect into realization and unbalancing the mind altogether.

─────── Mindfulness as Meditation ───────

Buddhism has evolved a wide variety of meditative techniques. The Hinayana or Theravada school of southern India sets great store on the path of *satipatthana* or way of mindfulness. Self-awareness takes on a literal meaning as meditation focuses upon the activities of the self: the breath, the body, the feelings and the contents of the mind. This is the Way of Mindfulness.

The concept of mind is central to Buddhist doctrine. The *Dhammapada*, a Buddhist text, begins with the phrase 'Mind precedes things, dominates them, creates them.'[20] Buddhist practice is about knowing the mind, shaping the mind and then freeing the mind. This process is achieved through the exercise of mindfulness. Its method is bare attention, its subject the everyday processes of mind and body. There are no external aids to attention, no devices, no images, only mindfulness.

Mindfulness begins with what is called bare attention, in which the attention is focused on the facts of perception through the senses. Bare attention consists in merely registering what is happening without judgement, preference or personal prejudice. This strips away the personal colouring that so often determines the way in which events are perceived and creates a clear and direct perception of the flow of life. Bare attention brings self-awareness and thereby self-control over thoughtless words, hasty deeds and the habitual patterns of thought and behaviour that make us prisoners. It teaches the individual to place awareness in the present moment, not to dwell in the past or live for the future. Pointless daydreaming, wish-fulfilling fantasies or nostalgia have no place. Bare attention will reveal just how frequently we resort to such escapist mental habits. Mindfulness places a spotlight in the mind which reveals the process of our daily thinking and shows just how scattered and fragmented our train of thought can be.

Bare attention is a very necessary preparatory stage in Buddhist meditation. It is possible to attempt a modified form of this by simply observing all personal interaction from a detached standpoint. Even a day of bare attention will prove revealing.

The practice of bare attention is complemented by what is called Clear Comprehension. This is the second aspect of Right Mindfulness. Clear Comprehension may be thought of as bare attention with the addition of comprehension of purpose and of actuality both internal and external. It therefore represents another dimension of attention. Awareness is no longer focused upon the sequence of events but upon the more abstract qualities of intent and action.

The practice of Clear Comprehension has four separate aspects within it; each is designed to extend self-awareness into another area of life experience. Clear Comprehension of Purpose requires that the individual should take time to reflect upon any proposed activity and decide whether it is in accordance with high personal aims and ideals. Clear Comprehension of Suitability requires that when faced with a choice of action the individual is able to select the choice which is most appropriate for the existing circumstances. This teaches adaptation and the ability to move with the flow of events rather than offer personal resistance to the forces of change. The Clear Comprehension of the Domain of Meditation requires that the individual should constantly ask how best mindfulness can be practised within the ever-changing and

difficult restrictions of everyday life and its practical demands. This
keeps the student ever-mindful of the practice of mindfulness. The
Clear Comprehension of Reality is focused upon the notion of Not-
Self. The individual is asked to become aware of feelings, thoughts
and desires as being impersonal processes which are not evidence
of the existence of self as an entity. The practices of Bare Attention
and Clear Comprehension together form the Way of Satipatthana.

The application of mindfulness is focused on four different areas:
body, feeling, state of mind and mental contents. Each exercise is
applied in a threefold rhythm, first to one's self, secondly to others
and finally to both.

Mindfulness of the body begins by becoming mindful of the
breath, of simply breathing in and out. The process is just
observed, not altered or changed in any way. Even this simple
instruction is difficult to carry out as it is difficult to observe the
flow of breath consciously without interfering with it. Focusing the
attention upon the flow of breath has a calming and relaxing effect
which invariably extends into areas of everyday life. Daily
mindfulness of breath is quite difficult to attain. It sounds simple
and can easily be tried out as an exercise. In practice it is not easy
and requires concentration and a considerable degree of inner
awareness. The only task is that of following the natural flow of
breath mindfully. The attention should be fixed at the nostrils
where the air strikes and it should not wander from that point. The
meditator may notice that the breath is stronger in one nostril than
in the other. There is nothing wrong in this, and no attempt should
be made to change it. Only if the breath cannot be felt at all should
the meditator take a few 'hard', deliberate breaths in order to
begin focusing. Close observation should reveal the pattern of the
natural breath and might also reveal any sequence in the pattern of
observation itself. Diligent practice will enable the meditator to
sustain awareness for increasingly longer periods so that there are
finally no lapses in concentration.

Mindfulness then extends to the body, postures are observed
with a detached objectivity, bodily functions such as looking,
bending, moving, eating, sleeping, even excreting, are all observed
from a detached and uninvolved perspective. Awareness is also
focused upon the various body parts. Its aim is to counteract the
notion of the oneness of the body by focusing on its separate parts
and to break the illusion of the beauty of the body by focusing on
the bodily mechanisms and its impurities. The overall aim is merely

to break the close identification that we all have with the physical body. This process is taken a stage further when meditation takes place upon the decaying body parts undergoing dissolution. Traditionally such meditations took place in cemeteries where real bodies were taken as objects for reflection. Nowadays internal visualization and reflection are thought to suffice.

It was a Burmese monk, U Narada, who in this century revitalized the traditional Satipatthana method. Under his influence modern centres were established to teach mindfulness to both monks and laity alike. A typical course might last for one or two months. Practice commences with the recitation of the Threefold Refuge, in which the student 'takes refuge' in the Three Jewels of Buddhism: the Buddha, the Dharma (teaching) and the Sangha (spiritual community). This serves to orientate the student. Each day provides the opportunity for general mindfulness in which awareness focuses around the four postures: going, standing, sitting and lying down. This includes full awareness of any alteration in posture, including the intention to change it and any sensation arising from changing it. All routine activities such as washing, eating, dressing or even walking are undertaken mindfully, that is with full awareness including observation of movement sequences, thought processes and any feeling responses.

Such detailed attention tends to create a slowing down of all processes so that activities are undertaken almost in slow motion. The simple act of taking a single step takes on an entirely new significance. Attention can be focused upon either the threefold rhythm of lifting, pushing and placing the foot or upon a twofold rhythm of lifting, pushing and placing the foot. Those experienced in the technique of mindfulness even observe a sixfold rhythm. The threefold rhythm is used for mindful observation without a gap and the twofold rhythm is used when it is necessary to walk a little more quickly. We can easily see that complete mindfulness demands a higher degree of concentration and awareness.

In the main daily practice awareness is directed towards the slight sensation of pressure which is caused by the rise and fall of the abdomen. Attention is focused upon the physical process itself; a hand may be placed on the abdomen in the early stages to make the movement more perceptible. Stray thoughts or lapses in awareness are to be noted also. With practice lapses and breaks in awareness should lessen.

By now it should be obvious that mindfulness is no easy task. It is nothing less than a mental training programme of a very high standard. When the initial course has been completed the individual is able to use what has been learned in the outside world. Mental discipline, continuity of awareness and calmness of mind are valuable assets in any walk of life, circumstance or situation.

Mindfulness does not stop with the physical body but extends to cover mindfulness of feelings in which the sensation in its barest form is observed without judgement. In Buddhist psychology the term feeling signifies a pleasant, unpleasant or indifferent sensation of physical or mental origin. It does not really carry the same interpretation that we might tend to place on it. The method of Bare Attention serves to bring personal responses and reactions into consciousness. The Buddha's advice on the subject is to be found in the Pali Canon:

> How does a monk dwell practising feeling-contemplation? When experiencing a pleasant feeling, the monk knows: 'I experience a pleasant feeling'; when experiencing a painful feeling, he knows: 'I experience a painful feeling'; when experiencing a neutral feeling, he knows: 'I experience a neutral feeling' ... Thus he dwells practising feeling-contemplation on feelings internally and externally. He dwells contemplating origination-factors in feelings, or he dwells contemplating dissolution-factors in feelings or he dwells contemplating both origination and dissolution-factors in feeling. ... Independent he clings to nothing in the world.

Mindfulness extends to the mind itself in exactly the same way. The state of mind is simply registered for what it is. There is no attempt at analysis or deep personal introspection. The existing state of mind is simply registered, nothing more. This method is rooted in daily living. In its full form it requires tuition and guidance but it is perfectly safe for anyone to use as a guiding principle. Its message is clear and simple, be mindful, know yourself. Try to be mindful for only a day and see what you discover.

CHAPTER 4

LET MEDITATION COMMENCE

It is hoped that you are now sufficiently interested to try meditation for yourself. The meditative state can be reached by anyone prepared to make the effort, patiently and on a regular basis. The following guidelines will help to explain what you need to do as you start on the path of meditation and prepare you for any simple difficulties that you might encounter.

Preparation of Place

The place that you are able to prepare depends upon the physical conditions at your disposal. Ideally you require only a quiet and comfortable place where you will not be interrupted by others. This might be no more than a corner of a bedroom but that is quite sufficient. It is not the place itself that counts but what you are able to bring to it. With practice you will be able to meditate anywhere that you wish. The place you choose ideally should be regularly available to you, especially at the outset. The same place regularly used tends to act as a trigger to meditation and builds up an atmosphere that is serene and calm. Minimize possible distractions as far as possible; take the phone off the hook or it is bound to ring.

Some people find it helpful to prepare the place for meditation by lighting a candle or burning incense. Such things certainly add to the atmosphere of a room and serve to sanctify the space being used. They can also serve to delineate the meditation period by providing a definite opening and closing to the session. There is no harm whatsoever in such preparation if it suits your temperament. Merely make sure that such items are put away when not in use, leaving them around casually defeats the object of using them in the first place. If, however, you should find that you cannot enter meditation unless you have your cherished things about you, then it is time to break the pattern.

Meditation is a state of mind that you can enter into wherever you are. There is a great deal to be said for sometimes moving outside when possible to meditate in the lap of nature. It opens up the possibility of meditating upon your surroundings and entering into the natural rhythm of the landscape.

As you attempt to integrate a new pattern into your life be careful not to let it intrude where it is unwanted. Your family may not be sympathetic to your new interests. It is much simpler to retire quietly to your room with as little fuss as possible rather than draw attention to yourself with billowing clouds of incense and sounding gongs.

Preparation of Self

Your internal preparation matters a good deal more than any preparation of place. A certain amount of inner but quite simple preparation is important. Just as worshippers in many parts of the world remove their shoes to remind themselves symbolically that they are about to cross the threshold from the mundane to the sacred, so we need to remind ourselves of the same thing. The act of ritually washing is often used to draw the dividing line between the physical and the metaphysical. There is a great deal to be said for even the simple act of washing face and hands as a preparation for meditation. What matters is that there should be some acknowledgement of crossing a boundary from one state to another. The outer acknowledgement can be dispensed with as soon as an inner one has been internalized.

Meditation can be likened to a journey. The first stage of that journey is quite simply entering into a state of physical relaxation. In time this becomes automatic and immediate but in the beginning it should be treated as a stage in its own right. The aim of this process is to relax the body while bringing the mind to the point of being one-focused. This is also the time to shed any tensions of the day and particularly any unwanted emotional residues. The body can be relaxed quite simply by going through the following process. Do not treat it as a purely mental exercise or it will fail to be effective. You must ensure that the body experiences the feeling aspect of the process.

Relaxation Technique

Sit comfortably adopting a suitable posture for meditation. Internalize the following sequence by repeating each phrase in the mind, turn the attention to that part of the body indicated, feel the qualitative change and only then move on to the next stage. The aim of this stage is to prepare the body by releasing any tensions and to prepare the mind by creating an inwardly focused state. Both mind and body should be poised at the end of the exercise. The relaxed state we are aiming to produce in no way resembles the unwinding process that we might go through after a hard day at work. We are seeking to awaken ourselves inwardly, not put ourselves to sleep.

Relaxation Exercise

I relax the muscles at the top of my head.
I relax the muscles throughout my face and head.
I am beginning to relax.
I am relaxing the muscles in my neck.
I am relaxing the muscles of my shoulders.
I am beginning to feel quite calm and relaxed.
I am relaxing the muscles of my back.
I am relaxing the muscles of my front.
I am becoming calmer and more relaxed all the time.
I relax the muscles of my legs and feet.
I relax the muscles of my arms and hands.
I am becoming calmer and more relaxed all the time.
My body is calm. I am calm. I am at peace.

This should be mentally repeated slowly and with intent. Each phrase should be allowed to sink in and take effect. The process should not be rushed. With practice it will become almost instantaneous so that you do not have to go through the procedure. As you enter the relaxed state you will also quite naturally adopt both the correct posture and the correct form of breathing. When the relaxation is complete you are now ready to commence upon the subject of the meditation. But before you proceed it is a good idea to make a particular point of opening the meditative state. This can be done in many ways. It can be achieved by simply making an opening statement in the mind, 'I now open this meditation' or by utilizing a suitable mental image such as parting a veil within the mind. The same procedure should be repeated at the closing of the meditation. This may seem a little theatrical and even unnecessary but it serves to ensure that the quite different sense of reality experienced within the meditation does not spill over into daily life. The return to waking reality can sometimes be quite a shock. If you should feel a little disorientated the best thing is to have a warm drink and perhaps a biscuit. This helps to establish consciousness within the physical body and close down any higher centres that might have been stimulated.

Meditation is about you and the changing self that you will experience within. This process is fragile, beautiful, sometimes painful. Don't let what you have thought, felt and experienced slip through your fingers. Get into the habit of writing down your inner experiences in an orderly fashion, keep a meditation diary. In this way you have a permanent record of what has happened to you. The following format is simple and easily adapted.

DATE:

TIME:

STRUCTURE: (i.e. subject of meditation)

REALIZATIONS:

Your diary entries do not have to be lengthy, a basic summary is all that is required. In the traditional monastic life the pupil would report daily to a superior so that progress and difficulties could be expressed. Your meditation diary is the next best thing as you are probably unlikely to have a personal teacher to guide you.

The Role of Posture

The very word meditation conjures up the image of the cross-legged devotee. This is perhaps unfortunate as many newcomers fear that they will have to master this exceedingly difficult pose even before they can begin to meditate. This is simply not the case. The lotus posture, which is indeed the classic Eastern stance for meditation, is excellent for its purpose. The body is balanced and stable, the spine is straight and it can be maintained with ease for long periods once it has been mastered. However, the average Westerner will find it all but impossible unless he or she has been trained in the discipline of yoga. We tend to forget that Easterners sit this way as children. It therefore comes quite naturally. It does not come naturally to the average Westerner and it is not necessary for meditation, even if it is desirable where possible. The physical body needs to be comfortable and balanced if you are to sit quietly for any length of time. It is not conducive to meditation if you develop cramp or backache. Therefore where and how you sit are important. A soft chair will only encourage you to slouch and in all probability you will fall asleep, and a low-backed chair will cause you to loll gradually forwards as time passes. The ideal chair is a high-backed one which will support but not coset you. Comfortable armchairs and soft sofas are out as far as meditation is concerned.

The position most easily adopted by Westerners for meditation is often called the Egyptian position as it is frequently depicted in ancient Egyptian statues. The body is seated, the spine is held straight, the head is upright, the feet sit flat upon the floor, the hands rest usually upturned one upon each thigh. It is a very simple posture, really no more than sitting in an attentive manner. Correct posture learned at the outset will pay off in the long run. Sloppy posture prevents proper breathing which also hinders the flowing of the subtle energies. I have often observed that people who pay scant attention to posture at the outset of a meditation session invariably subside into a crumpled heap as the meditation proceeds. They inevitably have difficulty in recalling what they have experienced. So just as when you learn to drive, get into good habits right from the start.

The Role of Breathing

We breathe quite unconsciously, without giving it a second thought. This is of course perfectly natural. However, during meditation we are seeking to achieve a particular state of mind and the pattern of breathing will take on a new significance. We all know from experience how our own breathing directly reflects our emotional state. If we become angry or upset, experience fear or panic then our breathing changes instantly. In everyday life the pattern of our breathing mirrors our state of mind. In meditation we reverse this reciprocal relationship by establishing a breathing pattern that will help to create a state of emotional calm and serenity. A pattern of deep, regular, rhythmic breathing has been found to be the most conducive to establishing the mental calm of meditation. There are more advanced breathing techniques which are part of more complex meditations but these are beyond the needs of the beginner. It is quite often revealing to become aware of one's own natural breathing pattern, to see particularly where we breathe from, whether deeply from the diaphragm or in short shallow breaths. For those used to breathing from only the top part of the lungs deeper breathing can be quite a liberating experience.

The breathing pattern most commonly used as a basic form by both Eastern and Western schools is the Fourfold Breath. It is quite easily mastered, though it may take a little practice initially. With time it will become perfectly natural and automatic.

The Fourfold Breath

Breathe in with a deep but comfortable breath from the diaphragm to the count of four.

Hold the breath at the top of the lungs for the count of two.
Breathe out slowly to the count of four.

Hold the lungs empty for the count of two.
Start again.

Initially you may need to practise this. Do not overdo the exercise at first. Half a dozen complete breaths is quite sufficient for a practice session. Always aim for a smooth, flowing breath which moves without effort from one stage to another.

The newcomer may feel that such exercises are a lot of fuss about very little – after all we all know how to breathe as we do it all the time. However, it is important to realize that we are beginning to use the breath in an entirely different way for a specific purpose. The East has done a great deal to reveal and codify the various effects of different forms of breathing upon the subtle bodies and the energy centres. The techniques of *Pranayama* which is the science of the applied breath, are very ancient and extremely powerful. Controlled breathing in varying patterns produces distinct effects upon the subtle life energies. The breath itself is a subtle manifestation of the life force and its power to create radical change in the body's system should not be underestimated. The fourfold breath is quite sufficient for basic meditation. It is easily mastered and provides a stable foundation for inner work.

———— Some Common Difficulties ————

You are now ready to commence meditation. At the outset it is wise to prepare yourself for any problems that might arise. Such difficulties are likely to be quite trivial but are often commonly shared by people starting out in meditation.

When Will I Find Time to Meditate?

In the beginning it often seems very difficult to establish a daily routine. After all you are now adding something to your life and it may prove difficult to find a slot for it. Short but regular sessions are far better than long but irregular ones. Ten minutes a day is fine initially. You might like to build up to between fifteen and twenty minutes at a later stage. You may find that you need to reorganize your living pattern slightly to accommodate a meditation period. Some people choose to get up a little earlier, watch a little less television or even use a lunch break. Unfortunately there is no easy answer to this problem. We all lead very busy and full lives. But where there is a will there is a way. It is worth knowing, too, that if you meditate regularly you will probably come to need less sleep and will be more efficient in everyday life, so that the time spent meditating will be made up for in these ways. For now, let meditation be incorporated slowly and gently into your life so that it is never obtrusive or threatening. This problem is the first obstacle, solving it is the first task.

Am I Really Meditating?

People often wonder if they are 'doing it right'. This worry seems to arise as a result of the mystification of the meditation process by some authorities. Do not build false expectations and you will not experience failure. If you have followed the steps outlined then you are beginning to achieve the meditational state. Meditation is a gentle, almost imperceptible process. The powerful states that you might have read about only come after experience and practice. Such experiences are in any case not to be sought. Be patient, change is not going to happen overnight. Meditation is a lifelong process, not a single event.

I Cannot Concentrate on My Meditation

This is a universal discovery. It is one of the reasons that we take up meditation. Unwanted and distracting thoughts can be very frustrating. This experience is part of the process itself. It helps if you do not get too involved in the unwanted thoughts. Let them pass by. Buddhists advise that you should recognize the source of your distraction even naming it: 'wandering, wandering,

wandering' or even 'itching, itching, itching'. This seems to prevent the distraction from becoming overwhelming. Eventually the distractions will lessen but initially they can seem quite formidable. Comfort yourself with the thought that every individual who takes up meditation experiences this stage. Do not allow it to stop you from continuing with your work.

*****

You now have all that you need for your journey. And every journey begins with a first step.

——————— Starting to Meditate ———————

It is now time to experience meditation if you should wish. Within any spiritual system, taking up of meditation is regarded as an important step. There is often a period of preparation which may take the form of strictly observing a particular code of behaviour and morality. Sometimes vows may be taken in the same way that a novice enters into the priesthood. Sometimes ceremonial is used to greet the new member into the spiritual life. All of these serve to remind the individual that a new step has quite literally been taken in personal terms. A threshold has been crossed. We might profit by the wise practices of our forebears in this and adopt a similar approach. It would be worth spending some time reflecting on why you wish to take up meditation. Are you ready and willing to be changed by the experiences that will be yours?

The following exercises each have something to offer. They are quite simple to follow. It would be wise to work with each one for a period of time rather than interchange them. It is difficult to say how long should be given to each, except to say that you will know when you have touched upon the inner experience and are ready to move on. Have the instructions close by. Read them through carefully before starting. It is helpful though not essential to read the descriptive journeys onto a cassette. Otherwise read them through first very slowly and carefully. You should be familar with the work on personal preparation and should be able to relax easily and be aware of both posture and breathing. It is also assumed that you will record each of the experiences as they happen.

Exercise 1. Locating Awareness

First establish deep relaxation by relaxing the body slowly and with intent. Become aware of the breath and its natural rhythm. There is no need to concentrate upon the breath in a deliberate manner; merely watch it gently moving through you. Place your awareness into the rhythm of the breath, allowing yourself to experience the rise and fall of the flow. Attune yourself to this flowing energy as it fills the body. Let your awareness expand to encompass the whole being. Attune your awareness to the experience of life within you which is everywhere. Be aware only of the feeling that this awareness brings. It is gentle yet vital. Stay with this feeling as long as you wish. Recognize this feeling within yourself. It is wordless and outside thought. It is the experience of the touch of your own true self. Each time that you return to enter this experience it will become more valid and meaningful for you.

Exercise 2. Experiencing the centre

Enter the relaxed state. Become aware of the breath and your own natural rhythm. Attune yourself to this flow by sharing its nature. Follow the breath inwards by allowing it to lead you. Enter the experience of the breath at a deep level. Harmonize yourself with its interior rhythm. Let it take you to a deep and special part of your own nature, to a place that expresses your own essence. Stay with the experience, share in the timeless quality that it has to offer. Immerse yourself deeply within the centre. Feel that this part of yourself radiates its essential nature out into space and time as far as you can conceive. It is boundless. It is infinite. With each experience of the deep centre, you enter into the reality of your own being. It then becomes possible to participate consciously as this vital quality is expanded and radiated out into the external world.

Exercise 3. Who am I?

Enter the relaxed state. Pose the question inwardly. Who am I? Answer thus: 'I am not my body.' Reflect upon the meaning of this phrase. Pose the question again. Who am I? Answer thus: 'I am not my emotions.' Reflect upon the meaning of this phrase. Ask the question again. Who am I? Answer thus: 'I am not my thoughts.' Reflect upon this statement. Finally pose the question again. Who am I? Answer thus: 'I am a centre of pure consciousness.' Meditate on the meaning of this statement.

It is possible and indeed helpful for beginners to divide this meditation into sections and meditate upon only one question during one practice. When all the separate sections have been meditated upon then the meditation should be used as a whole.

Exercise 4. Meditation on light

Light a candle. Sit so that it will be comfortable to focus on the flame of the candle. Become relaxed but keep the eyes open. Observe the flame. Come to know its qualities. Close your eyes. Take the image of the candle flame into the inner mind. Allow yourself to observe it in the mind's eye. Reflect inwardly upon its nature. Feel yourself being illuminated from within. Identify with the light in ways which seem meaningful to you.

Exercise 5. Following the breath

Establish a state of relaxation. Breathe naturally. Focus awareness on the abdomen and observe its rise and fall during each breath or upon the point within the nostril where the flow of incoming and outgoing breath can be felt. Merely observe the flow of breath without altering it consciously and without allowing the attention to wander. When distracting thoughts arise, be aware and gently bring the mind back to the focus of attention.

Exercise 6. Counting the breath

This exercise can be thought of as a continuation of the previous one. Be relaxed in yourself. Breathe naturally. Become attuned to the rhythm of inhalation and exhalation. Mentally count the breaths by tallying one for each completed breath. Count up to five whole breaths and then start again. Distractions will be especially noticeable in these two exercises. Aim eventually to be able to complete the practice undistracted.

Exercise 7. Exploring the circle

As a preparation take a piece of stiff card and using a compass describe a circle. Paint the circle with a colour of your choice. Place a dot at the centre. Establish a state of relaxation. Have the card before you at a comfortable distance. Gaze upon the circle and meditate upon its symbolic meaning. Close the eyes and internalize the circle. Hold the symbol in the mind and continue to meditate upon it. When your awareness is clear, project your mind into the central point and become aware of what you learn there.

Exercise 8. Encountering the tree

This is a meditation which utilizes the power of the creative imagination. It is helpful to record the created scene onto cassette by reading the text very slowly. If this is not possible it can be read through first very slowly. It is important to create and experience the images as being *real* in order to experience these meditations fully. Visual meditations of this kind are most frequently read aloud to an assembled group.

Establish relaxation within yourself. In your mind allow the place in which you find yourself to fade away. In your mind's eye find yourself standing outside in a meadow. It is early morning, the dew is still on the grass. Ahead of you in the distance standing against the horizon is a single tree. You begin to walk towards it. You reach the tree and sit down with your back against its trunk. From this position you are able to see how the roots of the tree extend like giant fingers reaching down into the earth. You run your hand over a nearby root reflecting that for the most part the roots are hidden. It is the roots which supply the tree with water and keep it anchored firmly in the earth. The roots are the foundation of the tree. You now stand and turn to face the tree running your hands over the bark, feeling the shape and texture of it. Look up into the branches. See the sky through the leaves. Watch the leaves and branches sway in the breeze. Here is the green crown of the tree. Amidst the leaves you perceive the still growing fruits of the tree which are also its seeds. When the time comes these will fall to the ground and each will have the opportunity to begin a new life. Each tiny seed contains the future tree within itself but as yet unrealized. As you stand before the great tree, wonder when it was seeded. How many winters has it seen? You draw closer to the trunk of the tree, embracing the living energy which is at the heart of the tree. Become aware of the powerful life force that flows within the tree. Rooted within the ground, reaching up towards the heavens, the tree is a living being. It breathes, feeds and takes nourishment. It produces offspring and eventually dies. It completes its own cycle, fulfils its own nature.

You remain within the scene reflecting inwardly until you are ready to leave. When you wish to depart, allow the images to fade.

Exercise 9. The rose within

Establish relaxation. Allow the room to fade. In your mind's eye find yourself outside under a warm sun. You stand in a garden of roses. It is a warm day. The scent of roses fills the air. About you roses bloom in abundance. You look about. There are roses of every colour and type. You will find your favourite here. You wander slowly among the flower beds taking in the exquisite beauty and delicate perfume. Some roses are in bud, others are fading and dropping. Still others seem to be at the peak of perfection.

You reach a bush of roses deep red in colour. Here the individual roses each seem to be perfect. You sit and gradually find yourself being attracted to one single bloom. It is as if you are seeing a rose for the first time. Its beauty and delicacy seem quite extraordinary to you. See how red is this rose, the same red as the life-blood. See too the thorns that stand guard. Let your mind enter into the individual bloom to experience its flowering and beauty. Feel how the rose opens to reveal its full beauty. Here is the creative power of love expressed in simple beauty. As you sit draw the image of the rose into yourself, holding it within the heart. Feel the rose within bringing its beauty and love into your being. Experience the opening of the petals within yourself. Experience what it brings to you. Be aware of the gift of the rose. Let others share in this gift also.

When you feel ready to leave your meditation allow the images to fade and return to waking consciousness.

Exercise 10. The lotus pool
Establish relaxation. Allow the place in which you find yourself to fade. In your mind's eye find yourself beside a small ornamental pool, seated beneath the shade of a young tree. It is a warm day. All is quiet and peaceful. If you listen carefully you will be able to hear the sounds of insects. Turn your attention to the pool. Sunlight glints on the water. Floating on the surface of the water you see beautiful white flowers similar in form and colour to lilies. You watch quietly, deeply absorbed by their beauty. You begin to wonder about these beautiful flowers before you. Allow your mind to drop beneath the waters, down into the mud where the lotus is rooted. You allow your consciousness to explore the bottom of the pool where the roots of the plant have their hold. These dark roots are quite unlike the fragile beauty of the bloom upon the surface. Yet here the plant draws sustenance and holds onto life. Allow your inner vision to rise following the plant's stem which moves gently to and fro in the water. This part of the plant is different yet again. Travel upwards following the lifeline of the stem observing that the waters are now becoming clearer. Here the sunlight

penetrates and the water is warmed. Rise up through the water until you again see the lotus which floats upon the surface. Its many petals are open to reveal its full beauty. How different is the flower from either the stem or the root of the plant. You have seen the root embedded in the earth and the stem drifting in the water. Now you perceive the delicate bloom which unfolds in the air in the heat of the sun. You have seen the three separate parts of the plant yet you have also perceived the wholeness of it.

Return to waking consciousness when you are ready.

Exercise 11. The butterfly

Establish relaxation. Allow this place to fade and in your mind's eye find yourself seated upon the grass in a pleasant garden. It is a warm day. About you there are flowers and bushes. You look about, enjoying the sights of the place. As you do so your attention is caught by a small movement upon a nearby bush. You get up to investigate more closely. You now realize that the movement was created by a small butterfly in the process of emerging. Watch spellbound as the tiny creature finally emerges from the cocoon case. You realize that you are sharing its first fragile seconds of life in this form. It begins to expand its wings allowing them to dry in the warm sun. Watch quietly as it prepares for its first flight. It is ready. It rises up on its fragile wings and disappears into the warm air. It is gone but you are happy to have witnessed its moment of birth.

Exercise 12. The path ahead

Establish relaxation. Allow this place to fade and in your mind find yourself standing upon a grassy plain. It is a vast expanse of open land. Ahead of you in the far distance is a mountain range towering and majestic. Its presence seems to draw and you begin to walk in its direction. Now you see that in the distance are other figures a long way ahead of you also walking in the same direction. You look behind and see a group of travellers in the far distance. You walk on a little more quickly spurred on by the knowledge that you are not alone on this vast open plain. The sun is hot. Continue to walk on, your eyes fixed on the goal ahead. You spend a long time walking. ... The land is now beginning to slope as you find yourself in the foothills of the mountain. The terrain is rockier and you have to pick your way with care. You sense a feeling of achievement now that you have come this far. The land is

beginning to rise quite steeply and you now have a clear view of
the plain beneath. You see small figures dotted over the plain.
Most move singly but some travel in small groups and you cannot
help but think of their good fortune as they walk together. They are
each heading for this peak and will in the fullness of time reach it.
You return you attention to your own journey and set out again
determined to travel as far as your strength will allow. You move
on with care picking your way over sharp stones. The journey is
more difficult now, the air is thinning and you are beginning to tire.
You pause to look up, the mountain looms over you. You feel
disheartened for a moment. There ahead of you is a good resting
place, a natural spot to sit comfortably for a while. You make your
way to it and sit and rest .... You now see that others have rested
here before going on ahead and made it a place in which to reflect.
From this place you perceive three paths each picked out by
previous travellers. On one side there leads a distinct track, quite
wide and well-worn. The stones have been cleared from it by
previous travellers who have prepared the way for you. On the
other side you pick out a less distinct path. It looks quite rocky and
steep but you can pick out a footprint in the earth so you know
someone has recently gone this way. You pause as you reflect and
look fully about. There pointing directly up the mountainside
someone has planted a staff in the earth. It points upwards but
there is no path at all to follow, just an indication that it is possible
to ascend by this route. You reflect on your position; you have
come this far. What will you do now, which path will you take? As
you sit wondering, a mountain mist begins to descend and rapidly
surrounds you.

Return to waking consciousness when you are ready.

*****

The next series of meditations are quite different in character. They
are based on the introductory subjects given in the Buddhist text
the *Visuddhimagga*. It is suggested that you take each meditation
for a definite period of time before moving on to the next. One
week is the absolute minimum suggested. You will have to make
that decision for yourself.

The Element of Earth
Take a small dish. Collect earth in it. Place this in a suitable spot.

Use this as a focus point for meditating on the Element of Earth. Let your mind expand to encompass the Element of Earth in its many forms and with its special qualities and properties. When you feel ready, project your own consciousness into the earth itself so that your mind is completely absorbed in it. Try to experience its nature and essence as fully as you are able. Withdraw your consciousness in a definite manner at the end of the session by becoming fully aware of your surroundings. Repeat this procedure throughout the period that you are working with the element.

The Element of Water

Take a small dish. Fill it with water. Place this in a suitable place and use it as a focus point for your meditation on the Element of Water. Dwell upon all the ways in which you have seen water and upon all the forms that it can take. When you are able, project your own consciousness into the Element of Water as far as you can. Be open to experience and inner perceptions. Withdraw your consciousness in a definite manner at the end of the session. Record your experiences and repeat this procedure until you have finished working with this element.

The Element of Air

Light a stick of incense. Place it in a suitable spot where it can act as a focus point for your meditation upon the Element of Air. Reflect upon the air and how we are able to perceive its presence. Recall its activities and powers. When you are ready project your mind into the Element of Air and become absorbed in its nature. Discover what you can through an act of identification with the element. Withdraw your consciousness at the end of the session. Repeat this format until you have finished your present work with this element.

The Element of Fire

Light a candle. Have it before you as your focus point. Reflect upon the power and forms of fire. Inwardly dwell upon its qualities. When you are ready join your mind with the Element of Fire as far as you are able. Discover what you can about its form and nature. Withdraw your consciousness at the end of the session. Repeat this procedure until you have finished working with this element.

The Circle of the Elements

Cut out a circle in card so that you can arrange each of the elements upon it. Place the dish of earth, the cup of water, the stick of incense and the lighted candle at each quarter. Arrange them so that the earth and fire are directly opposite one another as in figure 5. Meditate upon what has been created before you. Record your realizations.

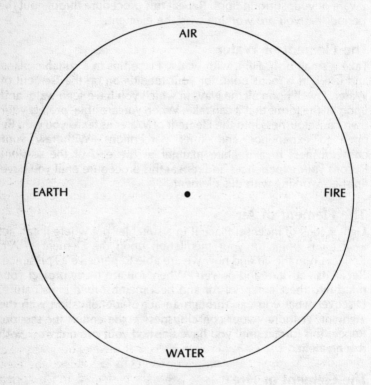

Figure 5

CHAPTER 5

THE HISTORICAL PERSPECTIVE

Meditation can take many diverse forms, yet beneath these different guises it is possible to trace some fundamental principles. Meditation appears in various ways in all the major spiritual systems of the world. Within each system, meditation takes on a particular colouring as a result of the framework in which it has developed. If we look at the main religions we find both esoteric and exoteric aspects. The exoteric aspect preserves the particular doctrines, ceremonial forms and outer appearances of the religion. The esoteric aspect enshrines the mystery of the living experience and will initiate those who come seeking. It is invariably within the esoteric aspect of the religion that we find the practice of meditation. If we look into each of the major traditional spiritual systems we will see the practice of meditation in operation.

Meditation in Christianity

Meditation tends on the whole to be overlooked by the vast majority of Christians. This is in many ways a loss to those seriously committed to the Christain faith. Personal meditation always has the power to bring philosophy and belief to life. Indeed the great Christian mystics and thinkers who have shaped the historical development of Christianity made spiritual practice the very core of daily life. The fruits of their labour have too often remained inaccessible and separated from the mainstream of Christianity. Meditation along with prayer and contemplation is part of the living spiritual heritage of the faith.

It was the group of men whom we now call the Desert Fathers who were the first to create a Christian spiritual discipline. They were the first of many Christian hermits who chose the harsh life of the desert in order to attune themselves more closely to the reality of God and the teachings of Christ. Their lives centred around Christian prayer, meditation and contemplation. Their simple wisdom and spiritual perception live on even today for we are still able to share their thoughts as preserved in the *Philokalia*. They could not know it but their lifestyle became a foundation for the life of withdrawal which others were to follow. Their meditations and prayers were obviously Christ-centred but the techniques employed were those that we find today around the world. We find detailed instructions concerning posture, breathing, the need for concentration and the power of inner visualization. Theophan the Recluse, one of the Desert Fathers, when writing about suitable posture for meditation states "Be like a violin string, tuned to a precise note, without slackness or supertension, the body erect, shoulders back, carriage of the head easy, the tension of all muscles orientated towards the heart."[21] Here we again discover the injunction to be relaxed and calm yet also alert. St John Climacus reminds us of the need for concentration within the practice of prayer. He says:

> Choose a prayer, be it the Lord's prayer or any other, take your stand before God, become aware of where you are and what you are doing, and pronounce the words of the prayer attentively. After a certain time you will discover that your thoughts have wandered; then restart the prayer on the words or the sentence which you last pronounced attentively. You may have to do that ten times, twenty times or fifty times; you may, in the appointed time for your prayer, be able to pronounce only three sentences and go no farther; but in this struggle you will have been able to concentrate on the words, so that you bring to God, seriously, soberly respectfully, words of prayer which you are conscious of, and not an offering that is not yours, because you were not aware of it.[22]

What he says of prayer applies equally to meditation and also to contemplation for the three are closely interrelated. What passes today for prayer is but one surviving practice from a range of more intensive contemplative exercises. We associate the word 'prayer' almost exclusively with petitionary prayer, which has never been part of mystical prayer. Petitionary prayer is essentially self-centred and is built around an exceedingly narrow and childish view of the relationship between the human and the Divine. Even when petitionary prayer seeks to bring healing or aid to someone else it is very often only a momentary act of closing the eyes and stating a request. Where is the internal recollectedness so basic to all spiritual activity? Where is the state of personal quiet beloved of all who discovered the mystery of living prayer? Where is the sense of inner contemplation so essential to interior reality? Petitionary prayer has nothing in common with spiritual practice.

It was the Desert Fathers who took the phrase "Lord Jesus Christ, Son of God, have mercy on me, a sinner" and created both a prayer and a meditation. It has become known as the Jesus Prayer and it is still widely used in the Eastern Orthodox Church. The Desert Fathers called it "the art of arts and the science of sciences" which is a mighty claim by any standard. Yet for them it had the power to effect a total transformation of the individual at all levels of being. It comes down to us by way of the *Philokalia*, the collected works of the early Christian Church, which has a great deal to say about the way in which the phrase should be used. St Simeon recommends:

> Sit down alone and in silence. Lower your head, shut your eyes, breathe out gently and imagine yourself looking into your own heart. Carry your mind from your head to your heart. As you breathe out say 'Lord Jesus Christ, have mercy on me. Say it moving your lips, or simply say it in your mind. Be calm, patient and repeat the process very frequently".[23]

In fact the aim is to use the prayer continuously according to the injunction of St Paul 'to pray without ceasing'. The prayer passes through distinct phases. At first it is verbalized; then it is repeated within the mind; finally it becomes a constant prayer of the whole being experienced within the breath and heartbeat itself. This simple prayer when used with intent as a meditation sums up the whole of Christian teaching. It affirms the reality of the Incarnation, the Divinity of Christ and the living relationship between the supplicant and the Divine Source. It is the Christian mantra. Its use as an interior prayer or constant meditation serves to anchor daily life within a Christ-centred framework. The Jesus prayer is a prayer of the whole being. It is centred at the heart and integrated at the physical level through the rhythmic breath. It is centred at the level of mind through constant repetition. It is centred at the level of soul through affirmation. The original Desert Fathers and all since, state that it should not be used except under the guidance of a spiritual teacher, as its effect is extremely potent.

Here we have an indication of the real purpose of Christian spiritual practice, to transform the individual totally and bring about the birth of the Christ within. This is always the aim of spiritual practice. The old self dies away and is reborn. The small self fades with the coming of a greater Self. The personality gives way to the true nature.

Christian meditation is no exception. To exchange inner practice for outer is to confuse the reality for the vehicle. Christian meditation can be powerful and transformative. It serves to explore and vitalize tenets of Christian doctrine and faith and confirm the relationship between the individual and his or her beliefs. It can be regarded as a loss that the techniques of personal and group meditation are not more widely taught for specific meditations exist within the Christian tradition. The spiritual exercises of St Ignatius Loyola are a series of exercises, both prayers and meditations to be undertaken over a period of four weeks as a retreat. In the introductory notes it states that just as

> Going for long or short walks and running are physical exercises; so we give the name spiritual exercises to any process which makes the soul ready and able to rid itself of all irregular attachments, so that, once rid of them, it may look for and discover how God wills it to regulate its life and secure its salvation.[24]

The exercises follow the life of Christ from the Annunciation to the Resurrection. It is a story that hardly needs retelling to any Christian, it is so familiar. Yet these exercises are designed to bring the text to life for the individual through the creative imagination. In the second week, for example the subject matter for meditation is the Nativity. The individual is asked to

> 'Represent to yourself in imagination the road from Bethlehem, in length and breadth. Is it level or through valleys or over hillsides? In the same way study the place of the Nativity. Is the cave spacious or cramped, low or high? How is it furnished? Look at the persons, our Lady, St Joseph and the servant-girl and after He is born the Infant Jesus'.[25]

The individual is then asked to respond personally within the scene. This technique is no different in principle to that used by the

Tibetan monk or the Hindu disciple. The exercises continue through the experience of the Passion and Crucifixion into the Resurrection in the same way, using personal visualization as a means of transforming individual consciousness. Such exercises tend to be overlooked by many Christians which is a pity. Meditative practice has a highly respectable history within the living faith of Christianity and are as important as shared worship and personal prayer.

In the Eastern Orthodox Church the icon still serves as a focus for the meditative state much as it has always done. The West has lost touch with this particular tradition probably as a result of internal divisions between the Church over matters of idolatrous practice. Those who make the mistake of seeing idolatry in the use of external symbolic forms confuse the vehicle with the reality, the form with the meaning. The icon has a long and worthy tradition. It is constructed as a consecrated item. The wood is especially chosen and blessed. The very paint itself is blessed. The icon painter follows ascetic rules during the painting procedure and paints from within the meditative state. The images depicted by the painter serve as a focus for meditation much as mandala. St John Chrysostom suggests that when standing before an icon the eyes should be closed and the image taken within as a focus for deep meditation. This is in principle exactly the same as using a mandala as a visual representation of certain qualities. The difference may lie in the fact that it is not obviously a symbolic representation in the same way as a mandala. However, the traditional forms that the icon painter uses do serve as symbolic vehicles. The traditional colour, gesture, stance, and even expression all serve to convey particular aspects of the Christian faith. The devotee does not worship the icon but through it realizes feelings of love and devotion. The icon is a focus point for spiritual aspiration and awakening for the Christian just as the mandala serves the mind of the Tibetan monk. The cross itself is an especially important focus for Christian meditation, but even more important is the Risen Christ, as the living pattern for life itself.

Meditation is the key to spiritual awakening. Without it any religious practice will become empty and devoid of meaning. This applies to Christianity as much as any other religion. When the inner life and the outer come together, worship becomes a living reality, doctrine becomes knowledge and faith becomes certainty.

———————— Meditation and Qabalah ————————

Qabalah is the esoteric face of Judaism. The word *Qabalah* is derived from the root *quibel* meaning 'to receive', indicating that this is a received tradition which is handed down from teacher to pupil. One tradition has it that the body of knowledge was received by the patriarchs through angelic teachings or through the otherworld figure of Melchizedek. Historically speaking Qabalah has its roots in sources and esoteric currents alive at the time of the birth of Christianity. It absorbed a strong Gnostic Greek influence and incorporated the emerging esoteric disciplines of Judaism itself. It seems likely that the teachings were preserved in a purely oral form for several centuries. Eventually it became part of the Jewish tradition and was handed on within small groups of Qabalists spread throughout Europe. Two texts became central to Qabalistic thinking. The Sepher Yetzirah or Book of Creation was extant in manuscript form in the tenth century and the Sefer ha Zohar which was written between 1280 and 1286 by Moses de Leon, a Spanish Jew. These two texts continue to exert a seminal influence right up to the present day. Qabalah became especially influential during the Middle Ages when it centred around Gerona in Spain. In 1492 there was an expulsion of Jews from Spain which forced Qabalah into a new and more public phase. It spread into Italy, North Africa and Turkey. There was considerable activity in Morocco in the fifteenth century. It spread and took root in Yemen and Kurdistan and centres were established in Aleppo and Baghdad. In the eighteenth century there was a particularly thriving centre in Jerusalem and in the nineteenth century there was a centre in Poland. Qabalah survives right up to the present day as a living and growing form of Judaic expression.

Qabalah is hard to pin down. It is intimately bound up with the Jewish people and their struggles and insecure existence. It has never put down permanent roots but ultimately been forced to move on either through persecution or dissension. Yet wherever it has travelled it has left its mark. There have been centres of Qabalah but these have been loose conglomerations of people, both students and teachers who created an atmosphere of cultural and spiritual activity. Such centres created spiritual and mystical literature, were a seedbed for Jewish consciousness and gave a temporary resting place for Qabalistic practice. The Qabalistic Jew is a devout Jew following all the practices and devotions normally ascribed to the Jewish faith. Qabalah, however, is an added dimension, in the same way that Sufism brings the quality of living spiritual experience to Islam. It has never been enshrined in a monastic or enclosed way of life, nor is there a founder or a set of clearly defined principles. It is a body of teaching which has developed through inspirational and intellectual writings. Its exponents have been scholars, mystics and teachers. Many devotional practices remain lost to us. If Judaic practice was frequently suspect in the eyes of other groups, esoteric practice was even more so. The image of the solitary alchemist surrounded by manuscripts and volumes is an image also of the Qabalist working privately through study, devotion, and meditative practice. Qabalistic teachings certainly inspired the practice of alchemy and became interwoven with Hermetic philosophy. This intermarriage created a new direction. Qabalah in this form became less concerned with its sense of Jewish identity and moved away from specifically Jewish religious practice. It gave rise to a development that might easily be called, Hermetic Qabalah. This blends much traditional Qabalah with the Hermetic philosophy derived from the figure of Hermes Trismegistus and the Emerald Tablets. Two esoteric traditions came together and gave birth to a greatly vitalized system of esoteric theory and practice which has become a foundation to students universally. Qabalah is no longer solely an expression of Jewish practice. It has become a guidebook for the genuine seeker, the aspirant who seeks to will, to know, to dare and to be silent.

Qabalah has been called the 'Yoga of the West'.[27] It offers a complete metaphysical doctrine and philosophy. It expresses teachings on the nature of the Divine, the nature of man and thereby the nature of reality. It also provides a completely practical system for inner unfoldment through personal meditation. Like any other spiritual system the Qabalah presents certain metaphysical concepts to the student through its texts. Qabalah, however, offers its students a perfectly unique method of teaching in the 'Otz Chim', the Tree of Life, not a text but a symbolic diagram. The tree may be thought of as a diagram of the forces operating within the universe. It is a multi-dimensional image which provides a personal map by which the student may be guided. It is simple in form but infinite in application. It is a means of internalizing knowledge so that each student becomes the living book itself. In the age of the microchip we are familiar with the idea that a great deal of knowledge can be encapsulated within a small space. The Tree of

Life can even be thought of in these terms. We need, however, to apply the right key to unlock what the Tree holds for each of us, otherwise we will not get access to the stored information.

Meditation is the major key for unlocking the experiences of the Tree. It is possible for the student to undertake the active experiences that the Tree has to offer by gradually working through its symbolic representations of universal laws. In this way the individual gradually experiences the pattern of unfoldment and growth inherent in the Tree. The emphasis is upon personal realization and inner experience, not intellectual appreciation. The Tree expresses a living reality which can be undertaken. The student lives the lessons of the Tree through daily life and in this way makes them a total part of consciousness.

The Tree of Life is depicted by a symbol composed of ten spheres with the addition of a hidden eleventh sphere. These are called sephira, and in the plural sephiroth. They are interconnected by twenty-two pathways (see Figure 6). The arrangement forms a composite symbol depicting the universal forces of both the macrocosm and the microcosm. The Qabalah teaches that before the process of manifestation commenced there was a state of existence known as the Great Unmanifest. Beyond knowing it is described in three phases: that of Ain, which is Negative Existence; that of the Ain Soph, which is the Limitless; and finally Ain Soph Aur, which is Limitless Light. From the three veils of Negative Existence the first point of manifestation proceeds which is Kether, the first sephira, the Godhead within manifestation. The process of manifestation proceeds in a series of ten stages or emanations which are symbolized by the ten sephiroth. Each is considered to be an emanation of the Godhead, and each is considered to be equally holy. The Quabalah teaches that there are four worlds. The first of these is the world of Atziluth, the World of Emanations which is the world of the Will of God. The second is the world of Briah where the Will of God takes on archetypal patterns. It is also said to be the realm of the Archangels as implementers of the Divine Word. The third of these is the world of Yetzirah the world of Formation where the creative patterns take up form. The fourth world is that of Assiah, the world of substance and action which is the material level. To illustrate this concept four trees are often drawn in the form of a Jacob's ladder one above the other. However, such complex metaphysical ideas are best reflected

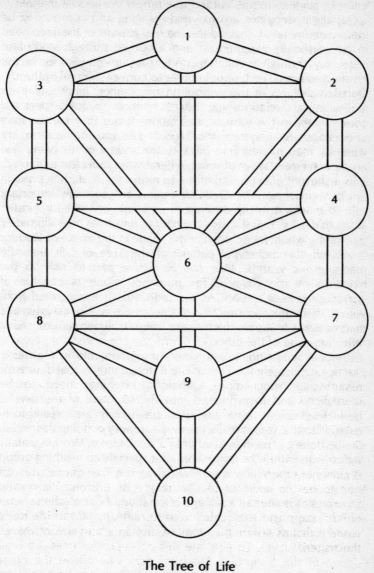

The Tree of Life

Figure 6

upon in meditation not learned in a purely intellectual manner.

Qabalistic doctrines are too wide-ranging and complex to be merely enumerated. Instead the internal lessons of the Tree need to be personally experienced and absorbed through study and especially through meditation. Whereas Sufism rejoices in the artistic and poetic metaphor in order to convey spiritual truths, the Qabalah delights in the symbolism of number, letter and even mathematical relationship. Such symbols require personal commitment in the form of meditation before they can be fully understood. As a system the Tree of Life provides a structure whereby man might climb back to the source of his being and finally enter the state of *devekut,* whereby the soul cleaves to God. This is the aim of every Qabalist – to return to the starting point in full consciousness. The Qabalah assigns an especially important role to mankind in the scheme of creation. It is not for himself alone that the Qabalist treads the path of return for he is ultimately part of the whole fabric. Mankind is made in the image of God for he shares the archetypal pattern of the Tree of Life with the macrocosmic worlds. Man has an active part to play in the structure of the cosmos, for humanity alone is capable of conscious self-realization. As the individual is transformed from within, that is microcosmically, so the cosmos is also realigned at a macrocosmic level, for the two are inseparably interlinked, being reflections one of the other.

Personal meditation plays a very important role in Qabalistic practice. Ultimately the Tree of Life is not an intellectual device for metaphysical speculation. Qabalistic teachings need to be internalized and incorporated into the structure of the psyche itself. Meditation upon the symbols which are traditionally assigned to the Tree is really the only sure way of doing this. Work can be done by the individual or in a small group. Work is usually undertaken within the framework of a specialized teaching group as personal supervision is very valuable. The Tree of Life will lead the student to experience the reality of universal laws and principles. It is after all an image of creation. It has eleven spheres which support the fabric of creation. Coincidentally mathematicians now tell us that we live in a universe of eleven dimensions!

Meditation in Buddhism

Buddhism in its varied forms makes much use of the practice of meditation. Indeed it could be said that the Buddhist philosophy itself came into being as the result of meditative practice. It was beneath the Bo tree that Gautama Siddhartha sat in long meditation and upon reaching enlightenment became the Buddha. The word 'Buddha' is a Sanskrit term which means 'fully enlightened one'. It is a term usually applied to one historical figure but it is also possible to think of a line of successive Buddhas reaching back into the past and stretching forwards into the future. After being enlightened the Buddha spent the rest of his life preaching and laying out a path that others could safely follow. He drew attention to the causes of suffering in the world and laid down the principles which lead to the state of liberation. He died at the age of 80 having brought a new spiritual path into existence.

Buddha established the foundations of the philosophy in his first all-important sermon "Setting in Motion the Wheels of the Law". In it he outlined the cause of all suffering, namely the graspings of the body, of sensation, of perception, mental phenomena and even of consciousness itself. Suffering, he maintained arises from clinging falsely onto that which is constantly changing and from falsely believing even in the permanence of self. His remedy to this was the establishment of the Noble Eightfold Path. This defined eight principles which, observed together, would lead to the termination of suffering. They are 'Right View, Right Resolve, Right Speech, Right Conduct, Right Livelihood, Right Effort, Right Awareness and Right Meditation'. It is a moral and ethical code for living. It is a philosophy and a daily practice. Buddha taught that when this way was followed it had the power to liberate from all material clingings, even to the wheel of Rebirth itself.

The teachings of Buddha gave rise to two main schools of practice. These are usually referred to as the Hinayana or Theravada and Mahayana schools. Theravada means the Doctrine of the Elders and its adherents claim that it represents the Buddha's original teachings. Historically it developed first. Its teachings are preserved in the language of Pali. It predominates throughout Asia. The Mahayana school evolved some four hundred years after the dealth of Buddha. It is found predominantly in Tibet, China and Japan. Its texts are predominantly Sanskrit. The term Mahayana means 'Great Vehicle' in contrast to Hinayana which means 'Little Vehicle'. The great vehicle carries the larger number of individuals to enlightenment. In the Mayhayana school the individual seeks enlightenment not for himself but as part of the enlightenment of all living things. The individual seeks to become a Bodhissatva whose purpose is the liberation of others. It even states that the historical Budda took the Bodhisstava vows aeons earlier under the tutelage of his twenty-fourth predecessor. In the Hinayana school the individual may only achieve personal enlightenment; there is no power to liberate others. The Hinayana school is always the more mundane, the Mayayana is always the more esoteric. Hinayana Buddhism perceives Buddha only as a man who made it possible for others to follow him to the enlightened state. Mayhayana Buddhism sees the Buddha as a projection of the Absolute. Each school has evolved its own traditions and practices. Meditation plays a central role in both schools.

It was Buddha himself who established the importance of meditation by making it part of the Noble Eightfold Way which are the eight precepts for Buddhist living. The last three categories of 'Right Effort'. 'Right Awareness' and 'Right Meditation' refer specifically to the establishment of personal mental discipline. In practice all eight precepts interact and overlap to create the Buddhist life.

The category of Right Effort (*samma vayama*) is defined as the effort to ward off unwholesome thoughts and produce wholesome thoughts instead. It requires a constant and clear perception into the mind at every moment. If we are not able to recognize the unwholesome thought as it arises, we will not be able to replace it by another thought. Its most important exercise is 'guarding the sense gates' in order to train for pure objective observation. In other words all interactions should be perceived with clarity. They should not be subjected to emotional distortion or personal bias. The emphasis on seeing things as they take place without personal identification is fundamental to Buddhist practice.

The category of Right Awareness (*samma sati*) refers to the practice of mindfulness. This practice aims to focus consciousness within each living moment. It demands concentration and a high level of awareness. The practice of mindfulness commences with attunement to the rhythm of the breath and is later extended to being mindful of the body, the feelings and the contents of the mind. It has become the main meditative practice in Theravada Buddhism. The principles, however, are fundamental to all Buddhist practice.

The category of Right Meditation (*samma samadhi*) refers to both the techniques and specific exercises to be undertaken. Buddhist texts provide a great deal of information about meditative practice and constantly emphasize the need to train the mind. The natural untrained state of the mind is considered to be one of ignorance and confusion. Buddhist practice is always about overcoming this. Right meditation is the final category and in many ways represents the culminating activity of the Buddhist way of life. It is certainly the key activity within Buddhism. It is not confined to monks but is recommended for all those attempting to follow the Noble Eightfold Path. Buddhism offers a variety of meditative paths and meditative forms. The path of concentration is a method of training the mind so that it can attain successively deeper levels of samadhi. The experience of this path is designed to serve as the foundation for other forms of meditative experience. It offers eight levels of concentration and experience for the meditator to explore. The basic levels are essential requirements for all inner experiences though the higher level are rather more specialized. This path does not, however, end in the goal of Nirvana and is therefore considered to be secondary to the path of insight. It is a means of training the mind not the route to liberation.

The next category of meditation is that of contemplation (*anupassana*). Deep reflective thought on the actual tenets of Buddhist Philosophy is here advised. The purpose is to bring the individual into close contact with the experiential reality behind the textual conceptions and to deepen understanding of Buddhist thought. Any of the major tenets of Buddhism provides suitable material for personal contemplation.

The last category is that of the Four Divine Abidings (*brahma-vihara*). The meditator enters a particular state of mind which is then radiated outwards. The individual experiences the qualities of loving-kindness, compassion, joy and equanimity which are then sytematically radiated out through the six directions. The aim is to suffuse the whole being with the dynamic power of the particular quality so that it is a total experience not purely a mental exercise. These meditations are often jointly practised by a group. The *Mettasutta*, the *sutta* of loving-kindness continues to be used throughout Asia on a daily basis in this way. Behind this practice lies the belief that such mental projections actually have the power to work for the good of others. Here is a positive assertion of goodwill which utilizes the combined channels of the mind and the heart.

Buddhists also share a devotional meditation often called the Recollection of the Triple Gem. It is brief in form.

I take refuge in the Buddha.
I take refuge in the Dharma (teaching).
I take refuge in the Sangha (spiritual community).

It should be used as a meditation. Each phrase is focused upon in turn. Its use should evoke feelings of devotion to the Buddha, to the path of enlightenment and to the brotherhood of Buddhists both past and present. It is a key meditation for Buddhists everywhere. This meditation is often used to open a session as a means of orienting the mind. It is often followed by a meditative exercise in which the individual progresses mentally over the entire surface of the skin then moves on to explore the flesh beneath, and finally encounters the skeletal structure. The process is then reversed.

Buddhism has developed a wide range of meditative practices. This permits flexibility of approach and recognized differing spiritual needs. Buddhism itself has developed into many forms. This is regarded as natural organic growth and no contradiction is seen in the wide variety of practices. Theravada Buddhism has developed mindfulness as its main meditational method while Mahayana Buddhism has developed more esoteric techniques and practices. Buddhism is a broad and all-embracing philosophy. It has produced the simplicity of Theravada practice, the richness of Tibetan practice and the uniqueness of Zen. Each is different, each is Buddhist. Each draws upon the main tenets of Buddhist philosophy in its own way. Each system faithfully follows the principles established by Buddha through its own cultural needs and particular development. In every system meditation is the key practice to awakening.

Zen Buddhism

The practice of Zen Buddhism has taken on almost a cult following in the West, especially in America where it has rooted in foreign soil with outstanding success. Its direct and disciplined approach has a powerful appeal as an alternative to modern day American materialism. Zen offers one of the most enigmatic and potent forms of spiritual discipline anywhere. Its unique approach earns it a special place among spiritual traditions. Zen is a Chinese-Japanese branch of Mahayana Buddhism. It originated with the sixth-century Buddhist teacher Bodhidharma, who in a legendary interview with the Chinese Emperor Wu astounded his audience by both his audacity and interpretation of Buddhist teaching. The Emperor was a devout Buddhist who had built temples and supported monks in order to further the cause of Buddhism and asked 'Now what is my merit?' Bodhidharma replied 'None whatsoever.' When the Emperor asked 'What is the first principle of the Holy teachings of Buddha?', Bodhidharma replied, 'Emptiness not Holiness.' Finally, when asked 'Who then now confronts me?' Bodhidharma replied, 'I have no idea.' This extraordinary exchange was a turning-point in the development of Buddhism; a new school of thought was born. Bodhidharma's replies were marked by the kind of logic that has now come to characterize Zen thought; the answer that is not an answer, the riposte that transcends the rational and confounds the mind into awakening.

Zen's main practice is *zazen*, that is sitting. This is performed on a daily basis. Practitioners sit facing a wall upon a cushion or folded blanket. In zazen right posture is considered to be of great importance for it expresses the right state of mind itself. The full lotus is commonly adopted and it symbolizes a state of unity in which mind and body are as one. The body is held upright and it should be possible to draw a line from the centre of the forehead, down through nose, chin, throat and navel into the coccyx at the tail of the spine. Correct posture is essential as meditation periods are often quite lengthy. Every part of the body needs to be balanced. Incorrect balance in one area will create strain and tension in another. In zazen the hands form the 'cosmic mudra'. The left hand is rested within the right, the middle joints of the middle fingers touching and the thumbs also lightly touching. The thumbs are held at the navel with the arms held slightly away from the body. There is a completeness and symmetry about the classic Zen stance. When it is correctly experienced it is easy to understand why it is said that when posture is right, the practice is right.

In zazen the mind is focused on the breathing, nothing else, so that consciousness is focused – yet paradoxically it is also expanded beyond all limitations. Breathing in is performed by inflating the lower abdomen; breathing out is effected by contracting the abdominal muscles. The rib-cage is kept as still as possible. This results in drawing on the residual lung reserves to give very deep expiration. In zazen attention is initially focused on the breath through the exercise of repeatedly counting the breaths. There are three ways of doing this. In the first both inhalations and exhalations are counted. When you inhale count 'one' and when you exhale count 'two', and so on up to ten. Then begin again. In the second method only the exhalations are counted from one to ten, the inhalations are passed over. In the third method the inhalations are counted and the exhalations are passed over. The first method is by far the easiest as experience will demonstrate. In Zazen we may obtain a state of *samadhi* in which consciousness ceases to focus upon any object and simply is itself, pure undifferentiated and still. Practice is regarded as the direct expression of realized human nature itself. When practice is pure, without expectations even of enlightenment, without a goal even of progress, then we attain what we seek: to be our true selves.

Zen is full of paradox; if enlightenment is our goal, then surely we should seek it? Yet this is not the way of Zen. Enlightenment, *satori* will come when it is ready and not before. It may even appear to come suddenly but like a fruit it comes to maturity only after growth is completed. Though the coming of enlightenment may be instantaneous the process leading up to it is invariably gradual. Like any other act of birth the moment of delivery follows a long gestation. Enlightenment is the direct experience of reality. It is beyond the limitations of dualistic conditioning. It is Unity itself. Zen techniques actively precipitate this state. Within the teacher–pupil relationship the student undergoes experiences which may trigger the awakened state. Only the teacher knows the subtle combination of psychological stick and carrot that will bring the student to awakening. Zen's most famous tool for precipitating a breakthrough is the *koan* (see page 73).

Zen preserves the all important teacher–pupil relationship. The term 'Roshi' means 'venerable teacher' and is given to one who commands respect and reverence by virtue of age or knowledge. The term 'Master' is reserved for the one who has attained full enlightenment and lives accordingly. The relationship between teacher and student is unique. It is intense yet quite impersonal. The student has a daily meeting, the *dokusan,* which is quite unlike the personal seminar of academic life. A teacher might answer a student's question with only one or two words, a long silence or even a blow. Such is Zen. Philip Kapleau relates a personal experience which shows us the range of personal interaction between pupil and teacher. A monk had stayed up during the night to assist him during an intensive period of meditation. This assistance came in the form of an encouragement stick with which he was struck on the shoulder blades on the acupuncture meridians. At *dokusan*, when he was being ushered before the Roshi, the same monk suddenly struck him violently behind the ear. In pain and rage Kapleau turned and swung at him. The monk ducked caught him by the waist and pushed him before the waiting Roshi who cried 'Good, Good!' They were the first words of approval uttered to him. He had made a breakthough from intellectual awareness to total involvement. Kapleau remembers the incident and the monk with great affection and thanks.[26]

It sometimes comes as a surprise to find that Zen also has ceremonial and ritual forms along with various devotional practices such as prayer and the giving of offerings. These are an integral part of the way of Zen which is wholeheartedly Buddhist first and foremost. Group practices also include chanting the sutras which are the purported words of the Buddha or the sounding of extended mantras. Such experiences are rituals in themselves and are part of the total commitment of being to life itself.

Zen is perhaps best summarized in the words of its founder Bodidharma:

A special tradition outside the scriptures,
No dependence on words,
A direct pointing at man,
Seeing into one's own nature and the attainment of wisdom.

Zen cannot be understood except through the direct experience of its teachings. It defies description, and intellectual analysis merely falls into the trap that Zen is designed to bypass. Enlightenment is beyond description and beyond conscious understanding. It brings understanding that changes the total being. When Buddha was enlightened under the Bo tree he said, "It is wonderful to see Buddha nature in everything and in each individual." This is the way of Zen; to realize the Buddha nature in all things, to gain direct experience of the unity of life and to become one's true self.

Meditation in Hinduism

The term Hindu simply means Indian. It is therefore as much a cultural description as a spiritual one. India is a vast country of many groups. It is not surprising that Hindu practices can be widely divergent, even contradictory. Hinduism affirms One God as the primal creative source but it also contains a multitude of divinities which are still widely revered as personifications of cosmic powers. The complex and even contradictory aspects of Hinduism reflect the many and various threads which historically have come to be woven into its fabric. The Hindu faith incorporates both Buddhist and Tantric practices. It is rich in ritual observance and communal celebrations. Yet it also offers an ascetic path for the solitary traveller. Within the multitude of divine images and the vast variety of religious devotions we find the unifying practice of Yoga. The word yoga means 'to unite'. The practice of Yoga presents a total philosophy of life and being. Yoga enshrines the esoteric face of Hinduism just as Sufi practice enshrines the esoteric heart of Islam, and as Qabalah is the esoteric aspect of Judaism. There are several forms of Yoga, not merely the physical path with which we have become familiar in the West. Each arrives at the same goal by different means. Jhana Yoga is the path of the intellect through the balanced activities of study and meditation. Bhakti Yoga is the path of love and devotion. Karma Yoga is the path of service. Hatha Yoga is the path of physical mastery. Raja Yoga controls the mind and Laya Yoga brings union through the activation of subtle energies. The classic text remains the *Yoga Sutras* compiled by Patanjali. This is a collection of aphorisms which outline the ways and means of yogic practice. The sacred texts of the Hindus are the *Vedas* which include the *Up anishads*. Together these form the foundation for Hindu belief and practice.

Yoga is set against the background of Hindu cosmology. This affirms a primary creative force which is called Brahman. This alone is Absolute Reality. Brahman cannot be limited through our concepts, nor described through images. In the Brahma sutras, Brahman is described as 'that which proceeds the origin, the sustenance and dissolution of the universe'. The universe is brought into being through the activity of Brahman which is present in all things. Manifestation takes place through the descent of the spiritual impulse into increasingly denser levels of form until matter itself condenses. As form becomes more dense so Maya also extends an increasingly dark veil over our sight. In man the reflected image of Brahman is Atman, the divine spark. Here we have a parallel with Christian and Qabalist thought. The key for discovering these eternal truths at a personal level is meditation. It is a vital part of the inner way for the Hindu disciple. We find interesting parallels with other systems in the teachings of Yoga. In common with Buddhist teachings, the Yoga Sutras describe humanity as being in an enslaved condition. According to the teachings the cause of ignorance is fivefold; ignorance of our real nature, egoism, attachment, aversion, and the fear of death which makes us cling to life. The Hindu equivalent of the Noble Eightfold Path is embodied in the Eight Limbs of Yoga. These are the steps necessary to bring about liberation. They are Abstention, Observance, Posture, Breath-Control, Sense-Withdrawal, Concentration, Meditation and finally Contemplation. We can already see some parallels with Buddhist precepts. Here is a code of conduct, a moral and ethical pattern for daily life and a means of inner unfoldment. The last three stages apply directly to the mind. These last three are called the Inner Limbs of Yoga. We find the same pattern for the meditative life; the preparatory practice of concentration, meditation proper and its full ripening in contemplation.

The spiritual dimension has always been a vital aspect of Hindu culture. The Indian people have a long tradition of spiritual teachers, holy men, gurus and swamis. At the same time India has also produced a staggering variety of fakirs, miracle workers, and psychics. These are generally looked down upon, having given up the goal of liberation for the spectacular display of incidental powers. Psychic powers are universally regarded as distractions on the path. Hinduism has been remarkably tolerant of such indulgence.

Meditation has a long and varied history within Hindu practice. It takes many forms. We find the extensive use of both mantras and mandalas as meditative forms. We find meditations which employ visualization and meditations which do not. We find prayer as meditation and meditation as action. We encounter meditation in simple and also in highly complex forms. Hinduism in every aspect is eclectic and tolerant. Its *modus operandi* is to enfold a wide range of practices rather than refine only a few. The methods of Hindu meditation are the same as those of other systems, namely concentration, absorption and liberation; its forms are many.

Hindu metaphysics provides a rich and complex cosmogony in which mankind embodies the divine image. There is never any doubt about the spiritual nature of life. According to Hindu thought the physical vehicle is only the most dense expression of this. Spiritual discipline and inner awakening create the possibility of bringing other more subtle vehicles of expression into consciousness. The *Upanishads* name five vehicles of consciousness. They are termed 'sheaths', because they veil Atman, the divine reflection, as a sheath conceals a sword. In the same way that the physical vehicle serves the physical plane, each sheath is regarded as being a vehicle for the appropriate level of consciousness. Specific meditations have the effect of opening the higher levels of awareness so that gradually consciousness extends in an unbroken continuum from the physical through the sheaths of prajna and mind to the vehicles of buddhi and bliss. This is effected through the esoteric practices of Laya Yoga which deal in detail with activation of the subtle energy centres and the awakening of the Kundalini force. This branch of Hindu practice has certainly absorbed a large measure of Tantra in its development. It sets out to establish and document, in almost a matter of fact way, the spiritual composition of man. Laya Yoga offers its own system for spiritual unfoldment and self-realization. Whereas Hatha Yoga deals with mastery of the physical vehicle, Laya Yoga deals with mastery of the non-physical levels through particular practices and meditative techniques. It teaches that awakening can be brought about through an orderly and sustained process of inner construction. Where Zen applies pressure to create a breakthrough, the way of Laya Yoga is to slowly clear away inner debris and build the channel which will carry the flash of liberation. The subtle composition of the true nature is immensely complex. As the physical body is built around the skeletal system, so the non-physical sheaths are interconnected through a system of energy centres or *chakras*. The meditative techniques of Kundalini Yoga centre upon the activity of the chakras. The task of the aspirant in this tradition is the cleansing, the orderly operation and smooth running of these important centres. The chakra system interpenetrates all level of being from the physical to the most refined. At the outset the centres are invariably in need of refinement. The system might be thought of as a series of locks upon a canal. Initially they are out of phase with one another, slow in use from long neglect, some are sluggish others are fouled with debris. With realignment comes the creation of new levels of consciousness. With full operation the Serpent of Wisdom rises from the base of the spine penetrating each centre on its journey. Self-realization is achieved with the activation of the crown chakra, the thousand-petalled lotus at the top of the head.

The inner journey of the serpent is also the inner journey of the self as it rises through the instinctive levels of being to the higher centres of love and creative outpouring. This journey is brought about especially through the applied mental power of meditation. Each centre is traditionally described through a set of symbols. These portray the qualities and functions of each centre. Each centre has its own visual representation which might be used as a focus for meditation. The particular symbols give access to the inner experience of each centre and serve to activate the interior functions. The throat centre, for example is described in the following way. Its presiding deities are Sadashiva and Shakini. He has five heads and ten arms. His body is smeared with ashes. He wears a tiger skin and about his neck there is a garland of snakes. On his forehead he wears a crescent moon turning downwards and exuding nectar. His consort is Shakini. She has four arms, and five faces with three eyes each. She is white and wears a yellow dress. The petals of this centre are smoky blue with letters inscribed in crimson. The centre contains a snow-white triangle and an elephant also in white. The mantra for this centre is *Ham*. Such images remain closed to the rational mind. Yet in the meditative state these same images will convey the nature of this centre and instruct the student in its powers and functions. Each centre has its own images which are used in the same way.

Meditation is used to bring the student out of ignorance into knowledge. Within Hindu practice we probably encounter meditation in the widest possible number of forms. Those used within Kundalini Yoga represent only one particular system. Each form of Yoga has its own meditations to offer. There are many possible guises which meditation may take. Each serves the goal of uniting the self, yoking the previously separated parts into a whole again. It is used as a means of recreating man in the image of God.

Meditation in Sufism

Sufism is the mystical heart of Islam. It is the esoteric face of Islam enshrined deeply within the orthodox tradition. Once again we find esoteric practice deep within the exoteric tradition. Sufism is not separate or in any way outside the main body of Islamic practice. It is the way of *haqiqa*, the inner truth, not *shari'a*, the outward law. Nevertheless the two are intimately connected. Sufism is the living heart within the body of Islam. It is the inner experience of the teachings of the Prophet. In Arabic the term Sufism is derived from the root *'suf'* wool, which refers to the woollen robe worn by the earliest Sufis who set the pattern for a way of life still followed today.

Sufi practice has three major aspects: doctrine, initiation and the spiritual method. It is a total way of life. Sufi doctrine is wide-ranging. It offers teaching upon all the fundamental questions raised by man's existence. Doctrine covers the Nature of God, the nature of man and the nature of reality. It deals with these fundamental areas through a rich and detailed cosmology, a deep psychology, a total philosophy and a complete system of metaphysics. It has given rise to a powerful aesthetic movement in all the arts from music to poetry from calligraphy to architecture. It has shaped the development of education and been a powerful force in the development of the sciences. It is entwined throughout the historical development of all aspects of Islamic culture.

Sufi teaching proclaims the essential Oneness of Divinity and the unity of all existence. All Sufi practice is a direct expression of this primary fact. Devotional practice seeks to bring experience of this oneness into consciousness; all endeavour serves to celebrate it.

See but One, say but One, know but One,
In this are summed up the root and branches of the faith.[28]

The role assigned to man is that of the returning traveller walking the path of realization towards the Divine Nature. It is the Mystic Quest at the heart of all spiritual practices. The goal is *Fana,* annihilation of the self, and *Baqa,* subsisting in God. Sufism seeks the total transformation from the divided to the unified, from the imperfect to the perfect Man. It is the path of gradual release from the bondage of ignorance and illusion. It is the path of rebirth into the spiritual life.

Sufism, unlike some spiritual practices, has not lost its rite of rebirth, initiation. It remains a fundamental principle. The Sufi Master stands as representative of the prophet and through him of God. To take the hand of the Master is to take the 'Hand of the Divine'. Admittance into the Sufi life is only through the door of Initiation, just as entrance into the world is only through the womb. The rite of initiation marks the point of death to the old life with all its values and rebirth into a new life. It sows the seeds of discipleship within the aspirant and confers the gift of Divine Grace through the Sufi Master. Initiation creates a permanent bond between the Master and the disciple. It establishes the foundation for a lasting and powerful relationship in which the student offers total obedience and surrender and the Master offers the path ahead. The chain of Initiation rather like that of apostolic succession stretches back in time to the founder of the religion, the prophet Muhammed. In this way the aspirant is inducted into the living aspects of the faith.

The spiritual method is the means through which transformation takes place. It is the means by which the seed of initiation is nurtured and in the fullness of time bears a full bloom. It is the means of spiritual unfoldment. Its central practice is *Dhikr* and *Fikr*. Dhikr is the remembrance of God through the repetition of the Divine Names. This is the way of continuous interior prayer. In practice the Divine Names may be repeated out loud or silently, singly or in a group. The individual is seeking a new awareness and identity through this practice. The constant repetition of the Divine Names serves to establish the Divine nature of the self. Dhikr is repeated with total concentration and absorption of mind, body and spirit. It is not petitionary prayer but prayer as mantra. The projected sound is a vital aspect of the practice of invocation. It imbues the practice with the living qualities of vibration and resonance which are an integral aspect of the Divine nature. Its complementary practice is Fikr, appropriate meditation which serves to reorientate the individual and awaken the powers of the soul.

Sufi techniques of meditation range widely and utilize the universal techniques of concentration, total absorption and final realization. The Master decides upon the actual nature of the meditative technique according to individual needs. Each Sufi order may also have certain preferred material that is part of its own tradition. One brotherhood for example use an exercise in which the aspirant walks with eyes down watching the tread of feet upon the path. It is an exercise in concentration and mindfulness. Here the student quite literally observes his own feet upon the path. It is a powerful symbolic lesson for one just finding the Way. The symbolism of alchemy is interwoven into the fabric of the Sufi way through its historical connections. It is a favoured vehicle for Sufi teaching. Alchemy offers a powerful symbol system for spiritual unfoldment. The unregenerate soul is likened to lead. The

Universal Man is likened to gold. The student is actively treading the path of transformation from one state to another. Meditation upon the images and processes of alchemy creates a powerful internal force for change.

The student is gradually opened to the reality of the teaching through the inner experience of meditation upon particular evocative images. A favoured image for reflection is the rose, beloved of the prophet and a universal symbol of the unfolding beauty within the divine soul. The image of the Mystic Rose appears throughout Sufi poetry and mystical literature. Symbols are a potent means of awakening the inner life. Certain symbols convey cosmological truths, others convey psychological truths and still others are symbols of revelation. Sufism is rich in symbolic forms which can be rendered accessible through inner visualization. Perhaps the most beautifully developed symbol is that of the Gardens of Paradise. This includes four gardens which represent four stages though which the soul must travel on the inner journey. They are called the Garden of the Soul, the Garden of the Heart, the Garden of the Spirit and the Garden of the Essence. Each garden contains the archetypal symbols of fountain, tree and fruit. The individual can explore and respond to the interior landscape moving with experience from one garden to the next. The interior journey is a frequent initiating component on the path. It is found in several traditions. Perhaps it finds its most poetic expression in the particular form.

Sufi meditation takes many forms. Meditation is never an abstract activity but is always integrated into the whole activity of life. Inspired poetry, sacred architecture, musical form: all are expressions of the inner life. There is no sense of separation between meditation and life. It is all one. It is the essence of Unity. Everyday activities are given a special significance which makes them acts of meditation in themselves. Rug-weaving, calligraphy and geometry are all vehicles for the meditative state. There is hardly an ordinary activity which is not transformed into an integrated aspect of the whole Divine life. It is in this context that Sufi mysticism created a unique meditational form, the dance of the Whirling Dervishes. The order of the Whirling Dervishes is called Mevlevi. Its Patriach is the great Sufi mystical poet Rumi. The whirling ritual dance is a mystical expression of the relationship between man and the Divine. It is an image of creation, its circular forms are in constant motion. It is a celebration of life, the right hand of each dancer is upturned to receive Divine blessing, the left hand transmits it to the world. It is a dance of union, an experience of ecstasy. It is outside definition, explanation or analysis. It is a mirror of the Divine which we seek to become. Each dancer progresses through a series of inner images which lock the macrocosmic and microcosmic realities together in one profound and total experience.

Sufi meditation is most often active. It involves all levels of being not just the mind. Its forms are those which evoke a total response from the individual. Within Sufism the written word is important but the sounded word is paramount. When sacred literature is chanted the subtle reality of the word as a living power is revealed. This is dynamic living meditation which unites the mind, body and soul and focuses it upon but one thing, the Divine Word.

The word is of great significance to the Sufi. The poem, the symbolic tale and the allegory are all vehicles for spiritual realization. Spiritual realities which cannot be formulated in the restricted language of deductive reasoning, can be expressed through the evocative language of the poet. Rumi's poetry tells of the absolute love of God for creation. It is a love which is written in countless signs and in an endless manner of ways. To see the signs to become aware of the ways is to come to know the love of God. This is at the heart of the Sufi Way. It is the principle behind all practice.

CHAPTER 6

LET MEDITATION CONTINUE

The following series of meditations are based on the technique of creative visualization. It is assumed that you have already completed the previous series of work and that you wish to proceed further. It is also assumed that you are now in the habit of regularly committing your experiences to a diary and that you are able to meditate regularly. It is suggested that the following meditations be completed on a regular weekly basis. If possible the text can be prerecorded for your benefit. This is only a suggestion; it is by no means essential to do this.

Exercise 1. Week 1.
Begin with the circle of the elements that you built in the earlier meditations. Reflect on your life and discover four qualities of being that you feel could be strengthened or enhanced as part of your own unfoldment. Reflect with care on these qualities and the value of them. Record them in your diary.

Exercise 2. Week 2.
When your choice is made, write them out on paper. Draw a circle in card. Your next choice will be to assign them to the elements themselves. You might find it helpful to assign practical, mundane or down-to-earth qualities to the element of earth, qualities of feeling or enhanced sensitivity to the element of water, qualities of mind to the element of air and qualities of inner drive, purpose or strength to the element of fire. When your choice is made, place your four qualities, one in each of the appropriate quarters of the circle. Meditate upon this and record your realizations.

Exercise 3. Week 3.
Allow this place to fade and in your mind's eye find yourself

standing beneath the dome of an ancient temple. Before you, laid out in the floor is a circle of gold inlay. The floor itself is marble and it is cool to the touch. From the centre of the dome on a long chain hangs a lamp which gives out a gentle light. You are standing just outside the circle inscribed in the floor. You wait. In one wall just beneath the dome there is a small window no more than a slit. It admits a ray of light and shows you the direction of the East. You ensure that you are standing facing East.

Take up a position on the circle facing outwards. You find that you are now standing before an altar. It is covered with a white cloth and upon it burns a single candle. There is also a chalice filled with deep-red wine. This chalice bears within it the source of the quality that you have come to seek from the element of air. You step forwards and take the chalice in both hands, saying as you do so, 'I seek the quality of .... May my efforts be blessed.' You now drink deeply of the chalice replacing it upon the altar when you have finished. Stand quietly before the altar meditating upon the quality that you seek ...

When you are ready, turn to your right, follow the golden band, and walk on until you reach the altar of the South. Here too a single candle burns, set upon a white cloth. Here stands a chalice which is quite different from the first. It contains the essence of that which you seek from the element of fire. You reach out and take it in both hands saying as you do so, 'I seek the quality of .... May my efforts be blessed.' You now drink deeply and replace the chalice when you have finished. Stand quietly meditating upon the quality that you seek here ...

Move on when you are ready, following the golden band until you stand before the altar of the West. As before the altar bears a white cloth, a lighted candle and a chalice. This chalice is different yet again and you spend a few moments observing it. Here within the chalice is the source of the quality that you seek from the element of water. You reach forwards and take up the chalice in both hands, saying as you do so 'I seek the quality of .... May my efforts be blessed.' You drink deeply and replace the chalice when you are finished. You stand quietly meditating on the quality that you seek here ...

Move on, making your way to the final quarter. You stand before the altar. Like the others it is covered with a simple white cloth. You see the lighted candle and the chalice which is unique in its own way. Here deep within the chalice is the source of that which

you seek from the element of earth. You reach out and take the chalice in both hands saying again, 'I seek the quality of ....
May my efforts be blessed.' You drink deeply, replacing the chalice when you are finished. Stand and meditate on the quality that you seek here ...

When you are ready make your way back to the starting point. Pause to reflect on your journey. Allow the images to fade when you are ready.

Exercise 4. Week 4.

Allow this place to fade and in your mind's eye find yourself standing beneath the dome of an ancient temple. Before you, laid out in the floor, is a circle of gold inlay. The central lamp gives out a gentle light. You ensure that you stand facing East.

Take up a position on the circle facing outwards. You seem to feel an enlivening force within as if you were standing upon a living current. You are standing before an altar as before. You see a lighted candle and a chalice upon a white cloth. Beyond the altar you see a pair of pillars reaching upwards, between them hangs a veil of gauzy fabric. Step forward and take up the chalice observing it as you do so. Draw it towards yourself. You recall the quality that you sought here and you silently meditate upon it. ... You take up the chalice saying as you do so, 'I offer the quality of .... to all who are in need of it from me. May my efforts be blessed.' As you stand there become aware of a living current which passes from you and then out through the veil into the realms beyond. Replace the chalice when you are ready. Move on by following the golden band.

Stand before the altar of the South. Beyond it see a pair of pillars which support a veil. Step forward taking the chalice in both hands observing its details as you do so. Draw it to yourself recalling the quality that you sought here previously. ... Step forward lifting the chalice in both hands saying, 'I offer the quality of ... to all who are in need of it from me. May my efforts be blessed.' Become aware of the living energy which embodies this passing out though the veil to what lies beyond. When you are ready move on by following the golden band.

Stand before the altar of the West observing what is before you. Here you see the lighted candle on the white altar-cloth and the chalice of clear crystal. Beyond the altar are the twin pillars reaching skywards. Between them hangs a veil. Take the chalice in both hands recalling as you do the quality that you came here to seek. Meditate upon it. .... Lift up the chalice saying, 'I offer the quality of .... to all who are in need of it from me. May my efforts be blessed.' Again become aware of the living quality passing out through the veil as a stream of radiating light. Move on making your way to the final quarter.

Stand before the altar of the North. Here too burns a lighted candle beside a chalice. Beyond the altar see the twin pillars towering up, the veil floating between them. You step forward taking the chalice in both hands remembering the quality that you came here to seek. Meditate upon it. ... Raise up the chalice saying, 'I offer the quality of .... to all who are in need of it from me. May my efforts be blessed.' Feel the quality of the living force passing through the veil and out into the world. Replace the chalice upon the altar when you are ready.

Make your way back to the starting point. Pause to reflect on your work. Allow the images to fade when you are ready.

Exercise 5. Week 5.
Allow this place to fade and in your mind's eye find yourself standing in the Temple of the Elements. See the circle of gold set into the floor. The central lamp gives out a gentle glowing light. You stand facing East.

You are standing in front of an altar as before. You see the lighted candle and the Chalice of the East. You stand quietly before it and pay your respects in whatever way seems meaningful to you.

Move on when you are ready by following the golden band until you reach the altar of the South. You see the lighted candle and the Chalice of the South. You stand in silent meditation and pay your respects in whatever way seems appropriate to you.

When you are ready move on by following the golden band until you stand before the altar of the West. Here you see the lighted candle on the white altar-cloth and the Chalice of the West. Stand quietly here paying your respects as you see fit.

When you are ready make your way to the final quarter until you stand before the altar of the North. You see a lighted candle beside the Chalice of the North. Stand in quiet contemplation and pay your respects as you wish here.

When you are ready return to the starting point of the journey in the East and from here look directly in the centre of the circle. You perceive that an altar stands upon the central spot. You make your way to the central spot by a spiral route, drawing closer and closer to the centre as you move on. Finally you stand before the altar of the centre. Here on a white cloth stands only a single chalice which is covered by a veil. You stand in silent contemplation of this chalice which seems so different from the others. It seems to emit a light of its own. You stand before it contemplating its mysterious presence here. It seems to be a living force. You feel yourself awed by it yet strengthened and also purified. You stand before it meditating in your own way, deep in your own thoughts. As you stand here in silent contemplation the light from the chalice seems to grow brighter as if in response to your presence. The gentle light seems to envelop you in a soft mist. You stay within the light of the chalice for as long as you wish. ...

When you are ready, allow the images to fade.

Exercise 6. Week 6.
Allow this place to dissolve. Find yourself standing in the Temple beneath the great dome. The lamp is lit and gives out a gentle light. Before you on the floor you see the golden circle. You take up your place in the East facing inwards into the circle. Ahead of you at the centre of the circle you perceive an altar. You make your way into the centre by a spiral route. You now stand before the altar. Upon a white cloth there stands a small chalice, delicate to hold, small enough to lift in one hand. You look more closely and perceive lettering or inscription of some kind upon it and even if you do not recognize this you know instinctively that it bears your name. You reach out and take the cup. It is empty. You carry it with great care for it seems very precious to you.

You now return to the eastern quarter holding the cup that is yours. You stand facing outwards. Beyond you tower the two pillars of this doorway, the veil between them is gone and you look out. You perceive the coming of spring; the buds are breaking and there is a bright green haze on the trees. Flowers are pushing their way into the light. All seems fresh and new. There is a great sense of renewal and rebirth. You step forward so that you stand between the two pillars, and offer up your own cup in a spirit of receptivity. You address the living forces of this quarter by saying 'I offer my cup at the Doorway of Spring. May my offering be blessed.' You become aware of a living presence responding to you, answering your offered chalice. ...

When you are ready you may move on, making your way to the

next quarter, the Doorway of the South. You stand before this doorway, looking outwards between the pillars. It is summer, the corn is ripe in the fields, the air is hot, the sun is high in the sky. It is a perfect summer's day. You step forward so that you stand between the pillars holding out the cup that you have to offer. You again address yourself to the living powers of the quarter by saying 'I offer my cup at the Doorway of Summer. May my offering be blessed.' You wait quietly upon the response of the indwelling presence for your offer will be answered. ...

When you are ready move on to the next quarter. You reach the western quarter and stand before the two pillars which open out onto the early autumn. The leaves are dropping from the trees in showers of gold and russet. There is a chill touch in the air. You step forwards so that you stand between the portals and offer up your cup saying 'I offer my cup at the Doorway of Autumn. May my offering be blessed.' Become aware of the living presence that responds to you and answers your offering. ...

Make your way to the northern quarter. Find yourself standing before the twin pillars of the Doorway of the North. You peer out beyond the door. It is dark, for this is the Doorway of Winter. Snow covers the ground with an icy blanket. The trees are bedecked with white. All is quiet. You step forward so that you stand between the twin pillars. You offer the cup to the living forces of this quarter by saying 'I offer up my cup at the Doorway of Winter. May my offering be blessed.' Wait quietly as the living powers of the quarter respond. ...

Make your way back to the East. Return to the central altar by a straight route and replace your cup upon it with thanks.

When you are ready, allow the images to fade.

Exercise 7. Week 7.

Allow this place to dissolve. Find yourself standing in the Temple beneath the great dome. The lamp is lit and gives out a gentle light. Before you on the floor you see the golden circle. You take up your place in the East facing inwards into the circle. Ahead of you at the centre of the circle stands an altar. Make your way to it taking a spiral route. You now stand before the altar. Upon the white cloth there stands a small chalice, which you recognize. You reach out and take it.

You now return to the eastern quarter holding the cup that is yours. Stand facing outwards. Beyond you tower the two pillars of this doorway, the veil between them is gone and you look out. You perceive the first moments of dawn. A rosy sun is just breaking over the horizon casting light into the world. The light gathers as the sun rises and dawn is complete. All seems fresh and new. There is a great sense of renewal and rebirth. Step forward so that you stand between the two pillars, and offer up your own cup in a spirit of receptivity. Address the living forces of this quarter by saying 'I offer my cup at the Doorway of Dawn. May my offering be blessed.' Become aware of a living presence responding to you, answering your offered chalice. ... When you are ready you may move on, making your way to the next quarter. Stand before the portals of this doorway looking outwards between the pillars. It is noon, the sun is at its most powerful. It shines from directly overhead. The air is warm. You step forward so that you stand between the pillars holding out the cup that you have to offer. Address yourself again to the living powers of the quarter by saying 'I offer my cup at the Doorway of Noon. May my offering be blessed.' You wait quietly upon the response of the indwelling presence, for your offer will be answered. ... When you are ready move on to the next quarter.

Reach the western quarter and stand before the two pillars which open out onto the early evening. The warmth of the day has passed but there is still the touch of it in the air. Step forward so that you stand between the portals and offer up your cup saying 'I offer my cup at the Doorway of Dusk. May my offering be blessed.' Become aware of the living presence that responds to you and answers your offering. ... When you are ready you may move on, making your way to the northern quarter.

Find yourself standing before the twin pillars of the Doorway of Midnight. You peer out beyond the door. It is dark for the sun has long gone. Instead another light hangs in the sky. All is quiet. You step forward so that you stand between the twin pillars. You offer the cup to the living forces of this quarter by saying 'I offer up my cup at the Doorway of Midnight. May my offering be blessed.' Wait quietly as the living powers of the quarter respond to you. ... Make your way back to the East. From there make your way back to the central altar and replace the chalice with thanks. Allow the images to fade when you are ready.

Exercise 8. Week 8.
Allow this place to dissolve. Find yourself standing in the Temple.

Above you is the great dome with its central light suspended on its long chain. It is lit and gives out a gently glowing light. Ahead of you set into the floor is the great golden circle which now seems so much larger than when you first encountered it.

Take up your place in the East facing outwards. The space between the pillars is veiled once more yet you are still able to sense the living presence which abides here and is aware of you. On this occasion you have come neither to offer – that has been done, nor to receive – that is being done, but simply to stand in quiet contemplation of this place and its meaning for you. You stand before the Gate of the East deep in thought. ...

Make you way towards the next quarter. You stand before the Portals of the South. The way is veiled yet you again sense the presence of the South as a living force which is aware of you. You stand before the pillars using this opportunity to stand in meditation before the Gate of the South. ...

Move on when you are ready and make your way towards the next quarter. You now stand before the Portals of the West. A veil hangs between the two pillars. It rustles slightly as if to indicate that the forces of this quarter are aware of your coming. You stand before the Gate of the West in inner contemplation of what this place means to you. ...

Move on when you are ready. Make your way towards the northern quarter. You stand before the Gate of the North. The gateway is veiled to your sight. But you are still aware of the indwelling presence here. You stand in silence deep in your own thoughts. ...

Make your way to the starting point of your journey at the East. Begin your journey to the centre of the circle by the spiral route. You tread your path with measured step, aware that every step takes you nearer to the central point.

Finally you stand before the altar. There is only a white cloth upon it, but as you watch you begin to make out the form of a chalice which seems to hover in the air suspended between the worlds. It seems to be made of something other than matter, for it glows gently with an inner light. You step forward. Its light seems to glow more brightly and it seems to expand, very gently, in dimension. You stand perfectly still as the gentle light begins to encompass you. It is still changing its dimensions, growing gradually. You now seem to stand within it for it has grown to encompass you. It surrounds you with light. It is light itself. It illuminates your very being. You stand within the Great Chalice in deep meditation, knowing that this chalice ever exists and can always be found by those who seek. Its intensity is sublime, soon it will be time for you to withdraw to take your place again in the outer world.

When you are ready, allow the images to fade.

Exercise 9. Week 9.

Allow this place to dissolve. Find yourself standing in the Temple. Above you is the great dome with its central light which gives out a warm glow. Ahead of you set into the floor is the great golden circle which now seems so much larger than when you first encountered it.

Take up your place in the East facing outwards. The space between the pillars is protected by the angelic form of Raphael. You perceive this figure as being dressed in a flowing robe of yellow shot through with mauve flashes. You stand before the figure and may take this opportunity to enter into communication with the living protector of this quarter. You stand before the Portals of the East deep in thought. ...

Move on when you are ready, making your way towards the next quarter. Stand before the Portals of the South. The way before you is guarded by the mighty figure of Michael with sword upraised. You perceive this figure as being robed in scarlet shot through with green. You stand before the pillars using this opportunity to stand in meditation before the protector of this gate. ...

Move on when you are ready and make your way towards the next quarter. Stand before the Portals of the West. In front of you, filling the open doorway, is the angelic form of Gabriel, Archangel of the West. You perceive this figure as being robed in blue shot through with flashes of orange. A cup of crystal is held aloft, and from it flows living water. Stand in inner contemplation using this opportunity if you should wish to enter into communication with the protector of this quarter. ... Make your way towards the northern quarter. Stand before the Portals of the North. You perceive the figure of Auriel in shades of citrine, olive, russet and black intermingled, the colours of earth. You stand in silence deep in your own thoughts using this opportunity if you should wish to enter into communication with the living protector of this quarter. ...

Make your way to the starting point of your journey at the East.

When you are ready begin to journey towards the centre of the circle by the spiral route. You tread your path with measured step, aware that every step takes you nearer to the central point. Stand before the altar. There is only a white cloth upon it, but as you watch you begin to make out the form of a chalice which seems to hover in the air suspended before you. Its shape seems to coalesce in front of you until you are able to see it quite clearly. You stand in silent contemplation of what is before you, dwelling on what it means to you. As you watch, the light of the chalice seems to grow bright, a bright and radiant cloud envelops it. ... Watch carefully, observing inwardly remembering that the chalice is but one form of the Grail. The cloud begins to clear, and you now see that the chalice has been transformed. Before you lying upon the central altar is a babe newborn. You approach the child and find that the babe looks deep into your eyes with a knowing wisdom. You respond to the child in your own way. As you stand before the child you may take upon yourself the role of its protector, for who else is there? You wonder at what you see before you and realize that you are partaking in the Mystery of the Grail. You may stay as long as you are able in the presence of the child. You will know when the time has come to withdraw for then the images will fade.

Exercise 10. Week 10
Allow this place to dissolve. Find yourself standing in the Temple. It is filled with a warm light. The golden circle seems to have grown immeasurably and you spend a few moments reflecting on this. ...

Take up your place in the East facing outwards. The space between the pillars is protected by the angelic form of Raphael again. You may use this opportunity to enter into communication with the living forces of this quarter if you wish. Stand before the Portals of the East deep in thought. ...

Move on when you are ready making your way towards the next quarter. Stand before the Portals of the South. The way before you is again guarded by the mighty figure of Michael with sword upraised in protection. Use this opportunity to enter into communication with the living power of this quarter. ...

Move on when you are ready and make your way towards the next quarter. You now stand before the Portals of the West. In front of you filling the open doorway is the angelic form of Gabriel, holding a cup of crystal. Stand before the gateway in inner contemplation, using this opportunity if you should wish to enter into communication with the living forces of this quarter. ... Make you way towards the northern quarter. You stand before the Portals of the North. You perceive the figure of Auriel guarding this place. Use this opportunity if you should wish to enter into communication with the living forces of this quarter. ...

Make your way to the back to the starting point of your journey. Begin to journey towards the centre of the circle by the spiral route which is now familiar to you. Finally you reach the central point and stand before the altar. Stand silently as the central mystery begins to unfold before your eyes. A pinpoint of bright light hovers in the air. It begins to grow until it coalesces into the form of the Chalice of Light. As you watch, the light of the chalice seems to grow brighter. A radiant cloud envelops it. The shimmering haze begins to clear. The chalice has been transformed. Before you lying upon the central altar is a babe newborn. You approach the child and you may renew your promise to serve as its protector. You stand in quiet communication with the child. A bright mist begins to gather about the child. It is so bright now that the child is lost to your sight. There is only a radiant cloud. Now from the cloud a figure steps out, emerging as if from bright sunlight. You immediately recognize the figure and step forward into a loving embrace. The figure speaks. ... Listen and remember all that takes place. You stand in the presence of this figure for as long as you wish. You will know when the time has come to withdraw, for the images will fade.

Exercise 11. Week 11.
Allow this place to dissolve. Find yourself standing in the Temple. Everything is as usual. You feel joyous and expectant here.

Take up your place in the East facing outwards. You stand before the portals and see that the veil is drawn back. Beyond the door is a path leading away into the distance. You stand a while perhaps wondering who might be permitted to come this way. You are aware of the guiding and protective force of Raphael at this quarter close by. You pause for a while entering into communication if you wish. ...

Move on following the band of light until you reach the quarter of the South. You stand before the portals and again find that the veil is drawn back here too. Beyond is a path leading away into the distance. Again you find yourself wondering who might be permitted to travel this path into the Temple. You are aware of the living force of Michael close by. You stand for a few moments, entering into communication if you wish. ...

Move on until you reach the West. Stand before the portals. Here too the veil is parted to reveal a path winding its way into the distance. You are aware of the presence of Gabriel here extending the power of love and compassion. Again you wonder who might travel this path. You spend a few moments of your time here. ...

Make you way towards the North. Stand before the portals. Here also the veil is parted. Beyond you perceive a path leading away into the distance. You are also aware of the strength of Aurie guarding this place. Spend a few moments standing here wondering who might walk this path to the Temple.

Move on until you reach the East again and complete the first circle. Now you begin to journey towards the centre of the circle by the spiral route. Reach the central point and stand before the altar. Upon the altar is a chalice quite real and solid to the eye. You step towards it and take it in both hands uplifting it for a moment to ask for a blessing upon your work. As if in answer to your thoughts you feel and instinctively know that each of the portals is now fully open. The guardians stand watch over each gateway. ...

Through each of the doors there come a slow moving line of figures. They come slowly for they are not able to hurry. They are those in greatest need. They come patiently, drawing close to you now. You see their faces, as they wait. You give each a drink from the chalice. It will never be empty. Here is the starving mother and her child, give them to drink. Here are the sick in mind and body, the tormented and the oppressed, the frail and the feeble. Each is entitled to drink and receive. Here see before you suffering humanity in its many forms. Offer each of them what you can. Some may address you before they depart. Each will return the way they have come. Stand for as long as you are able until each has received. ...

Meditate upon what has transpired. For a few brief moments you have shared the function of the Grailkeepers. The Grail is always in need of those who are able to assist in this way. Meditate upon this. You will know when it is time to withdraw for the images will fade.

Exercise 12. Week 12.
Allow this place to dissolve. Find yourself standing in the Temple. All is as usual. The golden circle is now a great swathe of light.

Take up your usual place in the East facing outwards. Be aware that this might be your last visit here for a time. You have come to bid farewell. Stand before the Pillars of the East and the veil which hangs between them. It moves lightly as if an unseen figure had lightly brushed against it. Become aware of the guiding force which resides here. You stand in silent communication with the living powers of this quarter expressing your innermost thoughts. You may receive guidance of some kind if you seek it. Salute the powers of this place and know that you are known and cherished here. ...

Move on to the next quarter. Find yourself standing before the Pillars of the South. See the veil which hangs between them. Stand in deep and silent communication with the forces which preside. Reflect upon what has taken place here and what you have experienced. Salute the living forces of this quarter and be recognized in return. ...

Move on to the next quarter. Stand before the Pillars of the West. The veil shimmers before you and you know that this is a place of living power. Stand silently remembering all that has taken place here. Express your inner feelings for you know that they will be understood. Salute the forces of this quarter and feel that you are acknowledged and cherished here too. ...

Move on to the next quarter. Stand before the Pillars of the North. Here too the veil moves as if an unseen presence is close. Remember all that has taken place here. Meditate on what you have learned. Acknowledge the living forces of this quarter in your own way. Salute the powers here and know that you are known and cherished. ...

Move on when you are ready. Make your way back to the starting point knowing that you have completed the outer circle. Now make your way to the centre by the spiral route. Stand before the central altar. Above it and around it there glows a bright light. In the midst of this you perceive the form of a chalice which hangs in the air. You step forward into the light so that you are enfolded within it. As you do so you realize that the chalice is beginning to change in dimension. It appears to be growing, expanding and moving so that it begins to encompass you within itself. You find that you have become immersed within the chalice. It has grown to encompass you totally. You have entered into its centre. You float within the interior world of the chalice like a child in the womb for as long as you are able. ...

The experience of the Grail fills your consciousness. You are now a part of it, just as it has become a part of you. These experiences can never be taken away. They are yours for all time. Give thanks in your own way and finally withdraw when you are ready.

CHAPTER 7

INSPIRATION FOR MEDITATION

Newcomers to the practice of meditation are very often dismayed to discover that their initial enthusiasm wanes when they find themselves at a loss for suitable subjects for meditation. This is especially felt by students who are working without support from a group or teacher. It sometimes happens that a student will give up altogether at this point. This is a great pity as the problem is easily remedied. There should never be any difficulty in finding suitable ideas for meditation. Experience soon shows that meditation requires no set subjects. Every life experience can become part of the meditation. However, the new student often feels the need to establish suitable meditational material and this intention is laudable. The inspiration for meditation is around us all the time in every place and in every shape. Meditate with the flow of life and you will never be empty.

Music and Dance as a Source for Meditation

Music is a powerful and beautiful stimulus which works at a deep level. It has the power to generate emotion, rekindle long-forgotten memories and place the listener in a totally different interior world. Music perhaps more than any other art form has the power to create immediate mood and atmosphere. Its impact ranges from the subtle to the sublime. Different types of music create different psychological effects. Martial music has the power to hold together a group mind in a given aim, sacred music elevates the spirit while 'musak', so widely found in shops and restaurants, has the power to lull and divert attention. It is the capacity of musical sound to act upon our psychological state which makes it such a rich source of inspiration for meditation.

The exact way in which music affects us remains a mystery. The complex interplay of pitch, timbre, rhythm and tempo creates a flow of sound which has the power to dynamically affect us. We do not need to understand the mechanics of music to enjoy it. Music is a powerful vehicle for personal realizations. When used as a definite focus for meditation it can provide a liberating, even a cathartic, experience. Music can be put to several quite specific uses for meditation. It can be used to establish the relaxed state. This can be particularly helpful if difficulty is encountered with the technique of progressive relaxation. It can be used to provide a suitable atmosphere and create sound pictures for guided visual meditations or by contrast it can be used to stimulate spontaneous imagery. Music can also be used as a vehicle for experiencing transcendent mental states. The choice will be personal from classical to rock, from ethnic to electric. There is much to be experienced in every form of music.

Certain musical traditions actively embody principles and constructions which are designed to transform consciousness. Such music tends to be part of a wider spiritual discipline and cultural heritage. Indian music especially has a long sacred history. It evolved along particular lines to accompany ritual dance and portray mythic tale. It employs forms which naturally create a meditative state in the listener. The drone, the sustained sound is much like a mantra and effects consciousness in much the same way. The drum beat also has the power to change mood and consciousness through complex and precise rhythm. It may even work directly upon the autonomic nervous system. The gamelan, the sacred orchestra of Bali also employs particular traditional musical forms. Its counterpart is the musical accompaniment to the Noh play of Japan. The twelfth-century Japanese writer Zeami said that such music was designed to 'open the ear of the mind'. Here we have a powerful statement about the impact of music on the psyche. These forms of music belong to ancient theatrical traditions of spiritual performance in which the total environment is a ritualized meditation.

The use of music and sound for meditation is a fascinating modern progression in an ancient art. There is much to be explored and documented. All experiences in this area are bound to be subjective – which does not make them any the less valuable. Certain pieces of music are known to produce a particular interior state. Music therapy is now established. It has shown us how music has a direct relationship to mood. Mozart's Clarinet Quintet in A and Clarinet Concerto have proved successful as relaxation music. Bartok's Fifth String Quartet is often used to arouse feelings of inner violence and power which are then released through visualization. Brahm's First Symphony is used to enrich inner emotions while Bach's Brandenburg Concerto No. 4 in G has an impact upon the rational and logical mental processes. Such correlations are thought-provoking. What is it within the structure of a particular piece of music that touches particular aspects within the psyche so immediately? Sound is expressed as vibration. Different combinations of sounds will create different vibrational patterns. It was an eighteenth-century German named Ernst Chladni who experimented with sand upon metal discs and revealed how various violin notes created different patterns. He discovered that the disc resonates to the violin only in certain places by shifting the sand to those areas which are vibrationally inert. His work was pursued by Hans Jenny of Zurich who also used discs to observe the changing patterns created as pitch rose up the musical scale. Familiar natural patterns such as concentric rings, stripes, pentagonal stars, hexagonal cells and spirals appeared. Furthermore as the pitch of a sound is raised it produces a shifting series of patterns. Each pattern is expressed in two ways. The pattern which is created as the sand collects visibly is formed upon the inert areas of the disc, the background pattern which forms in between represents the living vibrational structure. Here is a profound paradox; what we see and take as reality appears as a result of an invisible vibratory pattern. Jenny called his field Cymatics – the study of the interrelationship of wave forms with matter. He developed his explorations still further with the construction of a tonoscope, a machine which translated sounds into its visual counterpart on a screen. He made the astonishing discovery that the mantra *Aum*, when vibrated correctly, produced a circular shape filled with geometric patterns of circles and triangles. In other words the vibrated mantra actually gives rise to its own yantra. If a single sound has the power to generate so complex a pattern, the kaleidoscope of shapes and patterns produced by symphony would be fantastic beyond words.[29]

Music quite naturally makes us respond in movement of some kind. We might clap, tap out the rhythm, move our feet or get up and dance. Dance is usually a spontaneous personal response to a musical stimulus. As such it is unstructured and free in expression. By contrast there is an ancient tradition of sacred and formalized dance which is still preserved to this day. The temple dance is as much an act of worship as any silent prayer. It originated at a time when storytelling through performance was an important means of transmission. The dance encapsulated the great themes of creation and the opposition between the forces of light and darkness. It revealed spiritual realities through mythical characters and archetypal tales. Such dance was a meditation form in itself. Dancers were especially trained from an early age. Their training was long and arduous. This tradition is still alive in Bali, where young girls begin training at the age of seven. Who can say how long it will survive? We still find ritualized dance in certain parts of the world among peoples who preserve an unbroken link with the past. It appears as part of seasonal celebration and festivity. Sometimes it is used as performance; at other times it is used for group participation. In either case it is a vehicle for personal and group realization. Some modern groups have tried to recapture the essence of sacred movement by experiencing dance as meditation. The circle is invariably used as a basis for group dance. The steps are simple, the metre slow. Participants enter the circle as they might enter a meditation; in an altered state of consciousness. Dancers find themselves experiencing the circular form, treading the circle of the year, walking through the zodiacal signs, participating in a universal mandala. One particular group has specialized in reforming the dances of ancient Egypt, using the preserved wall-paintings as a guide. In common with Indian dancing, the gestures and movements are ritualized and serve to tell stories of the interaction between men and the gods. The dance is an act of deep contemplation for the dancers and the audience. The Whirling Dervishes (see page 118) are perhaps the most famous of all meditational dancers. Here dance is used to experience a transcendent state as the dancer whirls on his own axis turning like a planet in space. The dance is an image of creation, an expression of the One Life, an act of mystical union.

Dance as meditation through movement can be explored quite naturally by anyone. The realizations that arise from the total experience of mind body and spirit harmonized with mystical form will be well worth the effort involved in trying out a new meditational form.

Poetry as Meditation

Poetry is a rich source for meditation. It lends itself perfectly to the expression of abstract and intangible ideas. It is a vehicle for portraying the human condition in all its many appearances. Poetry has the power to reveal and make plain subtle nuances of meaning which might be lost in another medium. It expresses the hidden thoughts of humanity, the deep universal longings and shared aspirations. Here is all the joy of being human, the love and the hatred together described and made real. Here are all the events of life, the experiences of everyday life seen with a new vision. The poet is always a keen observer of humanity, intuitive and able to give voice to unspoken thoughts and feelings. The poet might be thought of as the spirit of the age eternally renewed as each age finds its own expression. In poetry we will find our own hidden thoughts, our joys and sorrows our strengths and weaknesses. Our human condition is revealed for us to meditate upon.

Poetry opens the door of the creative imagination and intuition. It speaks directly in image, metaphor and symbol. It teaches not by instruction but through realization. It evokes mood, sustains feeling and provokes an inner response. It can be a vehicle of expansion and awareness. The depth of poetry lies somewhere behind the words. Words only convey meaning, they are not the meaning itself.

Poetry is such a rich source for meditative thought. A single image might provide material for a considerable time. A whole poem might provide ideas for several months of meditation. It is not an intellectual appreciation that we are seeking, even though this can be rewarding but an expansion of our own consciousness through the medium of words and imagery.

We often discover that we are able to identify with the feelings and experiences that arise from a particular poem. We are able to share a moment of wonder or inner realization with the poem, and the poet. Poetry is a very personal experience. What speaks volumes to one person may say nothing to another. Certain poets are noted for their mystical vision and such poets invariably provide a rich treasure. It remains for the student to discover for himself or herself which poets and poems have the power to speak directly.

Nature as Inspiration for Meditation

Nature provides the richest and most varied inspiration for creative meditation. Her treasures are easily available to anyone with eyes to see. The great beauty of the natural world has been a source of inspiration for poets, painters, musicians and artists of every kind from the first cave painters to the artists of present day. We do not have to be great artists to appreciate nature. We are all artists in our own way. We each have a relationship with the external world of nature. It is not always recognized and acknowledged. Everything we do from the clothes we wear, to the food we eat, to the colours that we choose to have around us expresses our own personal relationship with the natural world. Meditation will make this relationship a conscious one.

When we take things for granted we cease to see them at all. It is as if they have ceased to exist. They cease to have any impact upon our lives. When we fail to be aware of the changing face of nature our lives are grey, our senses dull and our minds deadened. Today's urban sprawl and industrial living make it especially easy to become isolated from the natural environment. The inner city child has little experience of wild open spaces or rolling hills. Urban life makes the need for contact with nature all the more pressing.

Simple natural objects such as plants, shells and stones, can have profound effects when used in meditation. They can serve as vehicles for deep realizations about our own lives and our relationship to a greater whole. Both Eastern and Western esoteric traditions maintain that even inorganic things have life and consciousness. Such a concept has to be experienced to be fully understood. It is quite obvious that a plant or a tree is alive but what about a stone or a distant star? There are many discoveries to be made by the individual who is willing to meditate with an open heart and mind.

It is no coincidence that the discipline of meditation often takes the elements of nature, usually earth, air, fire and water as introductory subjects. We find this in the early Buddhist text, the *Visuddhimagga* and it is still a practice which is widely followed today. The reason for this is easy to see; here are the building blocks of the material world with which we are familiar. The subject matter is tangible and accessible. The elements are part of our everyday experience. As we begin to work with these four aspects our actual relationship to them will be changed and made more conscious. This shift in awareness makes us more thoughtful and aware of the impact that our actions, both individually and as a group have upon the natural world. We discover that upsetting the subtle balance of the elements one to another disrupts the harmony of the whole. To re-establish balance is no easy thing. We will find that working on the elements brings a sense of unity. We may even in our mind's eye survey the spacious subatomic world and become aware of this amazing and wondrous level of reality. In the mind's eye all things are possible.

When we have awakened to the living presence of nature about us we will find that our realization will affect our behaviour and actions in everyday life. We become more respectful and caring of nature's gifts less demanding and shortsighted. The natural world is under threat in so many ways at the present time. When we are awake to the interconnectedness of all life we know that to destroy the bounty of nature is ultimately to destroy ourselves. This may seem to be only common sense yet how often in the past have greed and ignorance overcome even this.

Communities have legitimate demands to make upon natural surroundings and resources. This has always been the case. Peoples who depend on the land for their livelihood, like the American Indian have always taken great care to preserve a harmonious balance with nature. Their simple wisdom remains preserved in tribal custom and ceremony. But industrialized man's relationship to the natural world has been marked by callous disregard of anything but short-term needs and long-term greed. We are reaping the fruits of this now as pollution in its many forms takes hold. Like a fire-alarm sounding, the devastation of lakes and widespread deforestation of hillsides, has at the eleventh hour awakened group consciousness to the need to redress the balance of nature. New attitudes are now emerging in the form of ecological and environmental movements. There is more interest and concern generally for animal life. Perhaps we would no longer exterminate several million buffalo in the space of a decade for sport, or would we? Perhaps we might now wish to save the dodo if we could, as we now wish to save the whale. It is salutary to reflect on the number of species that have been hunted into extinction by the predations of humans. Were we to be fully conscious of our dealings with the world about us such devastations would be a thing of the past.

The urban dweller of the twentieth century has largely lost touch with the natural cycles of seasonal change. Monthly cycles are marked out by the wage packet rather than the moon. Seasons pass us by like external events. We have ceased to feel part of the flow of the year. It was once the custom to celebrate the changing seasons with festivities and merrymaking, and in some parts of the world such customs still survive. When the seasons are marked out we begin to have an awareness of a reality outside our own. We can identify with cycles of experience that are shared with others. We begin to discover a personal orientation in our own lives. We instinctively know when to plant, when to harvest and when to be silent and await the coming of new growth. We become more conscious of the changing face of nature throughout the year. We begin to be more aware of the cycles of nature.

There is much to be discovered about our own lives from meditating actively upon the cycles and patterns that exist in nature. We have much to gain from the cycle of death and rebirth that we see in the natural world. We are part of nature, when we lose touch with our part of the pattern we are in grave danger of losing touch with ourselves. The patterns of nature have much to offer as focal points for meditation. We can use the seasonal cycle, the cycle of the moon or even the changing face of the heavens to expand our own awareness of the greatest reality of the created world around us.

Our distant ancestors saw nature as the Earth Mother, giver of the gifts of life bestower of bounty. Such a belief created a respectful and loving response. For the most part we have totally lost this sense of dependence. Our ability to manipulate the forces of nature has brought arrogance along with advantage. The former approach may seem simplistic even naive to industrial man, but it fostered a genuine understanding of the interdependence of all forms of life. We forget this interdependence only at our peril. It is very valuable to meditate on nature as the Great Mother. There is much to be learned and we may discover that we are not so different from our ancestors after all.

The American Indians and the Aborigines still maintain this childlike contact with the earth. Their traditional teachings uphold the sanctity of the land and the living interrelationship between people and nature. Tribal knowledge and wisdom is preserved in custom and transmitted through ceremony and spiritual practice. Certain areas of land remain sacred, for it is here that the living essence of the land is welcomed and thanked. Have we something to learn here or is the gulf between the land and the city now too great ever to be bridged? All our material needs are met in the supermarket and by the finance house, but in the last analysis everything that we eat, wear, use and enjoy is derived from nature. We might like to think that we have achieved some degree of independence but to believe this is to be fooled yet again by the myth of separation. Do not hesitate to use the natural world to inspire meditation. You will be rewarded many times over.

_____ Symbols as Inspiration for _____ Meditation

A symbol is something that conveys a range of meaning which far outstrips the literal expression of the object. The object usually acquires meanings that are connected with its qualities and common functions. For instance an everyday object such as a table might symbolically express the idea of people coming together peaceably. If the table were to be a round table instead, we might encounter a whole new range of meanings. Certain symbols are universally understood. In other words the same symbol will evoke a very similar response from people regardless of cultural background. The sun, for instance, symbolically conveys ideas connected with the heart of life itself, the moon with those hidden and mysterious currents within our lives. Such symbolic associations merely derive from the character and functions of both sun and moon respectively. Certain symbols still convey very much the same meaning to us as to our distant forebears centuries ago. Such things do not change. The inner language of the symbol lives on. It has an inherent power to evoke a response from us. Its power lies in the fact that it speaks directly to the intuition by conveying in an immediate form what cannot be expressed in words alone. Spiritual truths which stand above the limitations of the literal word find more adequate expression within such symbols. Spiritual truths have always been expressed in symbolic form. Each spiritual tradition absorbs images and symbols which best suits its innermost teachings. These then become the vehicles by which the most sublime truths may be conveyed. Tragically this is all too often misunderstood. We mistake the vehicle of teaching with the object of worship. The ancient Egyptians, for example, did not worship beings that were part-man and part-animal, though the ignorant and uninformed might like to believe that. The Cretans did not worship a bull in a literal way, even though worship was literally paid to the bull figure. The bull symbolized certain spiritual truths and functioned as a vehicle for spiritual awareness. If we are unable to see symbol as a spiritual vehicle, we run the risk of doing a great disservice to both our forebears and those of other spiritual persuasions. If we are contemptuous of the symbolic forms of another spiritual expression we are in danger of committing the sin of *hubris*.

Symbolic images are obviously both important and rewarding as themes for meditation. Symbols speak directly to the intuition and awaken consciousness in a very powerful way. When a symbol is used as a focus for meditation it provides an opportunity for the mind to roam freely and make associations and connections with other symbols. Initially this tends to be a somewhat intellectual exercise as we remind ourselves of the associations that a symbol has for us. Meditation, though, will soon bring about a more direct insight and perception. To take a simple example: if we use a circle as a symbolic form we are quite likely to find ourselves thinking about the circular flow of life, the eternal round of cycles and possibly even The Wheel of Life. Deeper meditation will reveal other more subtle ideas. The symbol has the effect of instantly putting us in touch with concepts that express universal truths. The symbol serves as a form of shorthand. It acts almost like a code; we insert the appropriate key and a tremendous amount of data is released. Other shapes also serve as vehicles for intuitive realization. The square and the triangle can each be used as focus points for meditation. The sequence of a dot and a line followed by a triangle can also prove very rewarding. Geometric shapes such as the cube, icosahedron, tetrahedron, octahedron and dodecahedron may also lead to some surprising insights when used as symbolic triggers for the intuition. Not everyone finds such symbolism helpful as their mathematical nature imposes a barrier which is difficult to overcome. Mathematics might even be thought of as a symbolic representation of universal laws. It is a complete symbol system in itself.

There will never be a shortage of suitable symbols for meditation. They are with us all the time in a wide variety of forms. They are the universal language of every spiritual system that has ever been. To meditate upon a spiritual symbol with effect is to touch something within that system. It even becomes possible to penetrate systems long gone by working with their important symbols. The Egyptian *Ankh* (see figure 7) belongs to a culture long departed, yet as a symbol of life it still has something to teach. The philosophy of the Tao provides us with a profound depiction of the balancing of opposites through the complementary forces of Yin and Yang. The serpent has a long history as a symbol. We find it in Christianity where it is invariably cast in an evil light. This is much at odds with its older and universal role as The Serpent of Wisdom (see figure 8). Meditation might prove fruitful on this particular point. Another ancient symbol is the maze or labyrinth (see figure 9). It should come as no surprise to learn that mazes were in the past physically constructed for spiritual ceremony and ritual. Meditation can take us each to the centre of the maze and help us to find the way out again. The castle is another ancient symbol of

Figure 7   The Ankh — Key of Life

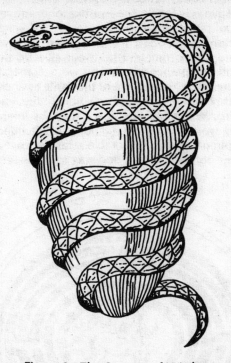

Figure 8   The Serpent of Wisdom

the self. It has a lot in common with the maze for we must explore each part of it and consciously experience its various chambers. There are many such symbols which appear throughout spiritual traditions. They should never be dismissed lightly. There is too much to be realized from meditating on them.

Each traditional spiritual system has produced its own symbolic forms which encapsulate its essential aspects. Meditating directly upon the symbol puts the individual in touch with the key teachings. Particular symbols are often held to have great transformative power and are not widely circulated. They belong to certain traditions which offer them to their own students as keys to inner awakening.

The person working without any group affiliation might easily take a universal symbol from the past and use it as a focus point for a period of time. Always choose a symbol which has never been used in a negative way (unlike the swastika for example, an ancient spiritual symbol put to negative use by the Third Reich). This can be a true learning process. We may even discover that our ancestors were not so different from ourselves in their spiritual aspirations and comprehension. When we become aware of the maze, the sacred tree, the serpent or the castle as ancient spiritual symbols we are beginning to awaken within to the inner power of symbolic forms. When we experience these as internal spiritual states of being we are using the symbol in its intended form, as a vehicle for spiritual truth. A veritable treasure trove of symbols awaits the keen student, each a doorway to the inner life.

From Montfaucon's Antiquities.

Figure 9   The Labyrinth of Being

GLOSSARY

Al Fana. Annihilation in God.

Anatta. The Buddhist doctrine of non-ego.

Anicca. The Buddhist doctrine of Impermanence.

Atman. The Supreme Universal Consciousness.

Avidya. Ignorance or incomplete knowledge.

Baqa. Subsistence in God

Bodhi. Supreme knowledge.

Bodhissatva. 'Wisdom Bearing'. One who has attained enlightenment and is dedicated to the enlightenment of others.

Brahman. The Supreme Universal Consciousness.

Buddha. A title meaning Awakened or Enlightened one. It is usually reserved for the historical person Siddhartha Gautama.

Chakra. A wheel or centre of force.

Dharma. Teaching; duty

Dhikr. The practice of 'remembrance of God' through the invocation of the Divine Names.

Fhikr. Appropriate meditation.

Jhana. Meditative absorption of the mind.

Mandala. A circular symbolic image which is used as a focus point for meditation.

Mantra. A word or sounded formula which is used as the focus of meditation.

Maya. Illusion, the phenomenal world as perceived through the veil of ignorance.

Moksha. Liberation from the Wheel of Birth and Death.

Mudra. Symbolic gesture used in teaching (usually in Buddhism).

Nirvana. The unconditioned state beyond birth and death that is reached after all ignorance and craving has been extinguished.

Nigama. The second of the Eight Limbs of Yoga: the five observances.

Prajna. Transcendental wisdom.

Samadhi. 'Putting things together'. The union of the meditator with the object of meditation.

Sangha. Spiritual community.

Satipatthana. The Path of mindfulness.

Satori. The goal of Zen Buddhism. A state of Enlightenment. Awakening to the truth lying behind duality.

Sherab. Higher Knowledge.

Sunyata. Voidness. The dynamic substratum of all existence.

Sutta. A sermon of the Buddha.

Vidya. Knowledge which is complete.

Vipassana. The path of Insight Meditation.

Yama. The first of the Eight Limbs of Yoga, the five abstentions.

Yantra. A symbolic geometric design used as a focus for meditation.

Zazen. 'Sitting Zen', in which the mind is stabilized, emptied and one-pointed.

NOTES AND REFERENCES

Introduction

1. See Alice Bailey, *A treatise on White Magic* for a more detailed explanation of The New Group of World Servers.

2. See P. Russell. *The Awakening Earth – Our Next Evolutionary Leap.*

3. The pioneering work of Kamiya in Japan in the 1950's focused upon the role of the Alpha rhythm in meditation.

4. See N. N. Das and H. Gastaut, *Variation de l'activite electrique du cerveau, et des muscles sqelettiques au cours de la meditation et de l'exstase yogique. Electroenceph Clin Neurophysiol* (suppl), 1955, 6:211.

5. See Barbara B. Brown, *Stress and the Art of Biofeedback.*

6. See C. Maxwell Cade and Nona Coxhead, *The Awakened Mind. Biofeedback and the Development of Higher States of Awareness.*

7. Chhandogya Upanishad III. xiv. 2.

Chapter 1. What is Meditation?

8. Roshi Philip Kapleau, *Zen Dawn in the West.*

9. Plato, *The Republic.*

10. Tarthang Tulku, *Openness Mind.*

11. Santideva, *Path of Light, Bodhicharyavatara.*

Chapter 2. Why Meditate?

12. See Thelma Moss, *The Body Electric.*

13. K. Walker, *A Study of Gurdjieff's Teachings.*

14. C. F. Andrews, *Letters to a Friend.*

15. William James. *The Variety of Religious Experience.*

16. Alban Krailsheimer, *Pascal.*

Chapter 3. The Techniques of Meditation
17. Thera Nanamoli, *Visuddhimagga, The Path of Purification.*
18. Chogym Trungpa, *Cutting Through Spiritual Materialism.*
19. Lawrence Blair, *Rhythms of Vision.*
20. Translation by Bhikku Kassapa.

Chapter 5. The Historical Perspective
21. Writings from the *Philokalia.*
22. ibid.
23. ibid.
24. *Spiritual Exercises* of St Ignatius.
25. ibid.
26. Roshi Philip Kapleau, *Zen Dawn in the West.*
27. Dion Fortune, *The Mystical Qabalah.*
28. *The Mystic Rose Garden.*

Chapter 7. Inspiration for Meditation
29. Lawrence Blair, *Rhythms of Vision.*

PICTURE REFERENCES

Figure 2. The Yurd Microcosm. Faegre, Torvald, *Tents, Architecture of the Nomads,* John Murray, 1979.

Figure 3. A Tibetan Buddhist Yantra. Ernest Wood, *Yoga,* Pelican, 1969.

Figure 4. The Yantra of Kali. Madhu Khanna, *Yantra,* Thames & Hudson, 1979.

Figure 6. Israel Regardie, *The Tree of Life,* Thorsons, 1975.

Figure 7. The Ankh. Manley P. Hall, *Secret Teachings of All Ages,* Philosophical Research Society, Los Angeles, 1962.

Figure 8. The Serpent of Wisdom. Hall, *op.cit.*

Figure 9. The Labyrinth. Hall, *op.cit.*

BIBLIOGRAPHY

Andrews, C. F, *Letters to a Friend,* Allen & Unwin (n.d.).

Anthony, Metropolitan, *Living Prayer,* Darton, Longman & Todd, 1966.

Arguelles, Jose and Miriam, *Mandala,* Shambhala, Boulder and London, 1972.

Aurelius, Marcus, *Meditations,* translated by Maxwell Staniforth, Penguin Classics 1985.

Avalon, Arthur (Sir John Woodroffe), *The Serpent Power,* Dover Publications, New York, 1974.

Becket, L. C. *Movement and Emptiness,* Stuart & Watkins, 1968.

Blair, Lawrence, *Rhythms of Vision,* Paladin, 1976.

Blakeslee, Thomas R, *The Right Brain,* Macmillan, 1980.

Bleakley, Alan, *Fruits of the Moon Tree,* Gateway Books, 1984.

Brown, Barbara, *Stress and the Art of Biofeedback,* Bantam Books, 1978.

Burckhardt, Titus, *An Introduction to Sufi Doctrine,* Aquarian Press, 1976.

Cade, C. Maxwell and Nona Coxhead, *The Awakened Mind,* Wildwood House, 1979.

Cartwright, Fairfax, *The Mystic Rose.* Watkins, 1976.

Conze, Edward, *A Short History of Buddhism*, George Allen & Unwin, 1980.

Cragg, Kenneth. *The Wisdom of the Sufis.* Sheldon Press, 1976.

David, Neel, Alexandra. *Buddhism, its Doctrines and Methods.* Bodley Head, 1977.

David-Neel, Alexandra, *Magic and Mystery in Tibet.* Abacus, 1977.

Doczi, Gyorgy. *The Power of Limit. Proportional Harmonies in Nature, Art & Architecture.* Shambhala, Boulder and London 1981.

Drury, Neville. *Music for Inner Space*. Prism Press, 1985.

Easwaran, Eknanth. *The Mantram Handbook*. Routledge & Kegan Paul, 1978.

Evans-Wentz, W. Y., *Tibetan Yoga and Secret Doctrines*. Oxford University Press, 1958.

Faegre, Torvald. *Tents, Architecture of the Nomads*. John Murray, 1979.

French, R. M. *The Way of a Pilgrim*. S.P.C.K. 1972.

Goleman, Daniel. *The Varieties of the Meditative Experience*. Rider, 1978.

Gyatso, Tenzin. *The Buddhism of Tibet and the Key to the Middle Way*. Allen & Unwin, 1975.

Halevi, Z'ev Ben Shimmon. *Tree of Life*. Rider, 1972.

Hall, Manley. P. *The Secret Teachings of All Ages. An Encyclopaedic Outline of Masonic, Hermetic, Qabbalistic and Rosicrucian Symbolical Philosophy*. Philosophical Research Society. Los Angeles, 1962.

Hamilton-Merrit, Jane. *A Meditator's Diary*. Souvenir Press, 1976.

Happold, F. C. *Mysticism: A study and an Anthology*. Penguin Books, 1963.

Happold, F. C. *The Journey Inwards*. Darton, Longman & Todd, 1968.

Hewitt, James. *Yoga and Vitality*. Barrie and Jenkins, 1977.

Hewitt, James, *Meditation*. Hodder & Stoughton. 1978.

Hodson, Geoffrey. *Music Forms. Superphysical Effects Clairvoyantly Observed*. Theosophical Publishing House, Adyar, 1976.

Humphreys, Christmas. *A Western Approach to Zen*. George Allen & Unwin, 1971.

Humphreys, Christmas. *Zen Buddhism*. Unwin, 1976.

James, William, *The Varieties of Religious Experience*, Longman, Green, 1902.

Johnson, Raynor C. *Watcher on the Hills*. Hodder & Stoughton, 1959.

Jung, Carl G. *Memories Dreams and Reflections*. Fontana Library, 1967.

Kadlovbovsky, E. Palmer, G.E.H. trans. *Writings from the Philokalia, on the Prayer of the Heart*. Faber & Faber, 1951.

Kapleau, Roshi Philip. *The Three Pillars of Zen*. Beacon Press, 1967.

Kapleau, Roshi Philip. *Zen Dawn in the West*. Rider, 1980.

King, Ursula. *Towards a New Mysticism*. Collins, 1980.

Krailsheimer, Alban. *Pascal*. Oxford University Press, 1980.

Leadbeater, C. W. *The Chakras*. Theosophical Publishing House, 1980.

Loyola, Ignatius. *The Spiritual Exercise of St Ignatius*. Anthony Clarke Books, 1973.

Luk, Charles. *The Secrets of Chinese Meditation*. Rider, 1984.

Merton, Thomas. *The Wisdom of the Desert*. Sheldon Press, 1974.

Mipham, Lama. *Calm and Clear*. Dharma Publishing, 1973.

Mookerkee, Ajit. Kundalini, *The Arousal of the Inner Energy*. Thames & Hudson, 1982.

Moss, T. *The Body Electric*. Granada, 1981.

Muktananda, Swami. *Kundalini, The Secret of Life*. Syda Foundation, 1979.

Nanamoli. Thera. *Visuddhimagga, The Path of Purification*. Berkeley. Shambhala, 1976.

Nasr, Seyyed Hossein. *Living Sufism*. Allen & Unwin, 1972.

Nyanponika, Thera. *The Heart of Buddhist Meditation*. Rider, 1983.

Plato. *The Republic,* trans, H.D.P. Lee. Penguin Classics, 1971.

Patanjali. *The Yoga Sutras of Patanjali,* trans by Dvidedi, Theosophical Publishing House, 1947.

Radha, Swami Sivananda. *Kundalini Yoga for the West*. Shambhala, 1981.

Regardie, Israel. *The Middle Pillar*. Llewellyn Publications, 1978.

Ropp, Robert. *The Master Game*. Dell. New York, 1968.

Ross, Nancy Wilson. *Buddhism A Way of Life and Thought*. Collins, 1981.

Russell, Peter. *The Awakening Earth – Our Next Evolutionary Leap*. Routledge & Kegan Paul, 1982.

Santideva. *Path of Light, Bodhicharyavatara,* trans. Lionel. D Barnett. *Wisdom of the East*. London, 1904.

Satprakashananda, Swami. *Meditation its Process Practice and Culmination*. Vedanta Society, 1976.

Scholem, Gershom, *Kabbalah and its Symbolism*. Schoken Books, New York, 1969.

Scholem, Gershom. *Jewish Mysticism*. Shocken Books. New York, 1967.

Scott, Mary. *Kundalini in the Physical World*. Routledge & Kegan Paul, 1983.

Sen K. M. *Hinduism*. Penguin Books, 1984.

Sekida, Katsuki. *Zen Training, Methods and Philosophy.* John Weatherill, New York, 1975.

Shabistari. *The Mystic Rose Garden.* Islamic Book Foundation. Pakistan, 1985.

Sinclair, Sir John R. *The Alice Bailey Inheritance.* Turnstone Press, 1984.

Siva Samhita. *The Oriental Book Reprint Cooperation.* New Delhi, 1975.

Slade, Herbert. *Exploration into Contemplative Prayer.* Darton Longman & Todd, 1975.

Slade Herbert. *Contemplative Intimacy.* Darton, Longman & Todd, 1977.

Steiner, Rudolf. *Knowledge of the Higher Worlds. How is it Achieved?* Rudolf Steiner Press, 1969.

Stoddart, William. *Sufism.* Aquarian Press, 1976.

Suzuki, Beatrice Lane. *Mahayana Buddhism.* Allen & Unwin, 1981.

Suzuki, D. T. *Living by Zen.* Rider, 1982.

Taylor, Gordon Rattray. *The Natural History of the Mind.* Secker & Warburg, 1979.

Trungpa, Chogyam. *Meditation in Action.* Stuart & Watkins, London, 1969.

Trungpa, Chogyam. *Cutting through Spiritual Materialism.* Berkeley, Shambhala, 1975.

Tulku, Tarthang, *Gesture of Balance.* Dharma Publishing, 1977.

Tulku, Tarthang. *Openess Mind.* Dharma Publishing, 1978.

Upanishads, The. Volume I. II.III & IV Bonanza Books, New York, 1952.

Van Lysebeth, André. *Prajnayama.* Unwin, 1983.

Walker. *A Study of Gurdiefff's Teaching.* Allen & Unwin, 1980.

Wood, Ernest, *Yoga.* Penguin, 1959.

INDEX

Absolute, The, 65
absolute *alaya*
    consciousness, 19
absorption, 29, 59
abstention, 113
activity, constant cycle
    of, 19
acupuncture, 42
Ain existence, 102
Ain Soph, 102
Ain Soph Aur, 102
air element, 93, 121
alaya consciousness,
    18–19
alchemy, symbolism of,
    117–18
alpha rhythm, 14–15
alpha training
    programmes, 15–16
Andrews, C.F., 149
ankh, 144
anupassana, 107
archangels, 102, 128,
    129, 130–1
'as above so below', 62
Assiah, world of, 102
Atman, 112, 114: *see
    also* Brahman
Atziluth world, 102
Aum mantra, 65, 69, 136
Auriel, 128, 130, 131
avidya, 19
awareness, 59, 75, 87:
    Right, 106

Bailey, Alice, 12, 26, 149

baqa, 53, 54, 116
bare attention, 75, 78
being, levels of, 69
Berger, Hans, 13
beta rhythm, 14–15
Bhakti Yoga, 112
bindu point, 65
biofeedback, 15, 16:
    training, 41–2
Blair, Lawrence, 150
bliss, 29, 114
Blundell, Geoffrey, 16
Bodhicharyavatara, 36,
    149
Bodhidharma, 109, 111
Bodhissatva, 35–7, 106:
    vows, 36
Book of Creation, 100
Brahman, 20–1, 112: *see
    also* Atman
Brahma Sutras, 112
brahma-vihara, 107
brain, during meditation,
    13–17
brainwave biofeedback,
    see biofeedback
breathing, 48, 62, 76,
    83–4, 88: counting the
    breath, 88; in *zazen,*
    109–10; limb of Yoga,
    113
Briah, world of, 102
Brown, Barbara B., 149
Bucke, Dr R.M., 54
Buddha, 105
buddhi, 114

Buddhism, 105–8:
    consciousness levels,
    18–19; Three Jewels
    of, 77; void, 21, 30;
    see also Bodhissatva,
    mindfulness, Zen
butterfly exercise, 91

Cade, Maxwell, 16, 149
cancer, 43
chakras, 114, 115:
    crown, 53, 70, 115
chalices, 121–6: *see also*
    Grail
chanting, 71, 111
*Chhandogya Upanishad
    III,* 149
Chladni, Ernst, 136
Chogym Trungpa, 60,
    150
Christianity, 95–9
Chrysostom, John, *see*
    John Chrysostom, St
Chuang-tzu, 23
circle exercises, 88
Circle of Elements, 94,
    120–2
circles, *see* mandalas
comprehension, clear,
    75–6
concentration, 28–9, 50,
    62, 107: difficulties in,
    85–6; limb of Yoga,
    113
consciousness: daily, 69;
    sheaths, 114; states of,

24–30; theories of, 18–19
constant cycle of activity, 19
contemplation, 107, 113
'cosmic mudra', 109
cosmograms, 63
Coxhead, Nona, 16, 149
creative imagination, 49–50, 59, 61, 88–9; exercises in, 120–33
crown chakras, 53, 70, 115
cymatics, 136

daily consciousness, 69
dance, 136–8
Das, N.N., 14, 149
death, meditation on, 34–5, 46
death-rebirth image, 61
de Leon, Moses, 100
delta rhythm, 14
Dervishes, 118–19, 137
Desert Fathers, 95–8
detachment, 45–6
devekut, 104
Dhammapada, 74
Dhikr, 71, 117
diary, 82
direct involvement, 24
direct perception, 25
Divine Mind, 20–1
Divine Names, 117
dokusan, 110–11
Domain of Meditation, 75–6
'doubt-mass', 33, 73
dream consciousness, 25, 26, 28
dreaming sleep, 69
dreamless sleep, 69

EEG, *see* electroencephalography
earth element, 92–3, 122
earthly Bodhissatva, 35–6
Effort, Right, 106

Egyptian position, 83
Eightfold Path, 105, 106
Eight Limbs of Yoga, 113
electroencephalography, 13–14
elements, 92–4, 139: circle of, 94, 120–2; temple of, 122–4
Emanations, world of, 102
emotional well-being, 43–7
enlightenment, 19, 35, 53, 73, 110
equanimity, 29
equilibrium, inner, 42
existences, qabalistic, 102

fana, 116
fear, 34
Fikr, 117
fire element, 93, 121
Formation, world of, 102
Fortune, Dion, 150
Four Divine Abidings, 107
fourfold breath, 84

Gabriel, 128, 129, 131
Gardens of Paradise, 118
Gastaut, H., 14, 149
Gavraud, Professor, 68
geometric shapes, 143
Godhead, 20–1, 102
Grail, 129, 131, 133
Great Beings, 36
Great Mother, 141
Great Unmanifest, 102

haqiqa, 115
hara centre, 71
Hatha Yoga, 112, 114
health, 40–3
Hermes Trismegistus, 101
Hermetic philosophy, 20, 101
higher knowledge, 19, 52

Hinayana school, 74, 105, 106
Hinduism, 18, 19, 20–1, 69, 111–15
Hui-Neng, 74
'hundredth monkey', 12–13

icons, 99
Ignatius, St., 59, 98, 150
individual consciousness, 18
inferior Brahman, 21
infinite space, 29
initiation, Sufi, 116–17
inner equilibrium, 42
insight, 29–30, 62, 107
intuition, 19–20, 143
involvement, direct, 24

James, William, 149
Jenny, Hans, 136
Jesus Prayer, 71, 97
jhanas, 28–9, 62
Jhana Yoga, 112
John Chrysostom, St., 99
Jung, Carl G., 61, 62

Kali yantra, 66, 67
Kamiya, 149
Kapleau, Roshi Philip, 35, 53, 110–11, 150
Karma Yoga, 112
kasinas, 57
Kether, 21, 102
Key of Life, 144
Kirlian photography, 42
knowledge, higher, 19, 52
Koan, The, 33, 73–4, 110
Krailsheimer, Alban, 150
Kundalini Yoga, 53, 114–15

labyrinth, 144, 145, 146
la ilaha illa Llah, 71
Laya Yoga, 112, 114
light, meditation on, 88
Limitless, The, 102

Limitless Light, 102
lotus, 69–70: pool
    excercise, 90–1;
    posture, 82–3
Loyola, *see* Ignatius, St.

Mahasattava, 36
Mahavairocana Buddha,
    60
Mahayana school,
    105–6, 109
mandalas, 62–5, 66
manifestations, process
    of, 102
mantra, 68–71, 97, 111:
    Aum, 65, 69, 136
mazes, 144, 145, 146
meditation: difficulties,
    84–6; exercises,
    86–92, 120–33;
    inspiration for, 134–46;
    nature of, 23–38;
    preparation for, 79–80;
    reasons for, 39–56;
    relaxation, 81–2; Right,
    107; spiritual way of
    life, 30–8; state of
    consciousness, 24–30;
    techniques, 57–78
meditative
    consciousness, 25, 27
Melchizedek, 100
mental well-being, 47–50
Mettasutta, 107
Mevlevi order, 118
Michael, archangel, 128,
    129, 131
mind, meditation and,
    17–21: *see also*
    consciousness
mindfulness, 30, 45,
    74–8, 106: of breath,
    48, 62, 76
Mind Mirror, The, 16–17
moksha, 53, 54
Moss, Thelma, 149
music, 134–6
mystical consciousness,
    25

mystical states, 53–6
Mystic Rose, 118
mythology, 61

Nanamoli, Thera, 150
nature, 139–42
negative existence, 102
Nirvana, 30, 107
Niyama, 31
Noble Eightfold Path,
    105, 106

observance, 113
Om Mane Padme Hum,
    69–70
onepointedness, 28, 29,
    48
Ouspensky, 45–6
Otz Chim, *see* Tree of
    Life

Pali Canon, 78
Paradise, Gardens of,
    118
Pascal, Blaise, 55–6
Patanjali, 122
path ahead excercise,
    91–2
Paul, St., 97
perception, direct, 25
personal experience, 25
personal mind, 20
Philokalia, The, 96–7
photography, Kirlian, 42
physical well-being, 40–3
Plato, 32, 65, 149
poetry, 138
postures, 76, 77, 82–3,
    109, 113
prajna, 19, 69
Pranayama, 84
preparation, 79–80
purpose, comprehension
    of, 75
Pythagoras, 65

Qabalah, 21, 71, 100–4
quest image, 61

Raja Yoga, 112
Raphael, 128, 129, 130
rapture, 29
reality, comprehension
    of, 76
Recollection of the Triple
    Gem, 108
relative *alaya*
    consciousness, 18–19
relaxation, 40–1, 43,
    81–2
release, 53, 54
Right Awareness, 106
Right Effort, 106
Right Meditation, 107
'right seeing', 20
root consciousness, 18
rose symbolism, 118
rose within exercise,
    89–90
Rumi, 118

Sadashiva, 115
samadhi, 73, 107, 110
samma samaadhi, 107
samma sati, 106
samma vayama, 106
Santideva, 36, 149
satipatthana, path of,
    74–8
satori, 53, 55, 110
seasons, 124–5, 141
seed mantras, 70
seed thoughts, 71–3
Sefer ha Zohar, 100
self-awareness, 18, 33,
    34
self-knowledge, 33, 34,
    45, 52–3
self-observation, 45
self-realization, 33–4, 35
sense-withdrawal, 113
Sepher Yetzirah, 100
sephira, 102
Serpent of Wisdom,
    114–15, 144, 145
Shakini, 115
sheaths, 114
sherab, 19, 52

Simeon, St., 97
'sitting', *see zazen*
sleep, 69
sound, 68–71, 134–6
spiritual way, 30–8
spiritual well-being, 51–6
Steiner, Rudolf, 26
storytellers, 60
substance and action,
    world of 102
Sufism, 71, 115–19:
    initiation, 116–17;
    symbolism, 117–18
suitability,
    comprehension of, 75
sunyata, 21
Supreme Brahman, 21
symbolism, 117–18,
    142–6

Tagore, Rabindranath,
    53–4
Taijasa, 69
tantra, 52, 114: yantra,
    65, 66
teacher-pupil
    relationship, 73–4,
    110–11
Theophan the Recluse,
    96
Theravada school, 74,
    105
theta rhythm, 14

thought, seed, 71–3
Threefold Refuge, 77
Tibetans, 14, 19, 59–60,
    63–4
trance consciousness, 25,
    26–7, 28
transcendent
    Bodhissatva, 36
transpersonal experience,
    25
tree: encountering the,
    88–9; meditation on,
    24
Tree of Life, 101–2, 103,
    104
Trismegistrus, Hermes,
    see Hermes
    Trismegistrus
Tulku, Tarthang, 149

U Narada, 77
Upanishads, 52, 112, 114

Vaisavanara, 69
Vedas, 112
vibrations, 68–71, 134–6
vidya, 19
Vipassana, see insight
visual meditations, 15,
    49, 57–62, 88–9
Visuddhimagga, The, 57,
    150,

void (Buddhist), 21, 30

waking consciousness,
    25–6, 28
Walker, K., 149
water element, 93, 121
well-being: emotional,
    43–7; mental, 47–50;
    physical, 40–3;
    spiritual, 51–6
Wheel of Life, 143
Whirling Dervishes,
    118–19, 137
wisdom, 19–20, 52:
    Serpent of, 114–15,
    144, 145
worlds, Qabalistic, 102
Wu, Emperor, 109
Yama, 31
yantra, 65–7, 136
Yetzirah, world of, 102
Yoga, 14–15, 112: Eight
    Limbs of, 113; *see also*
    individual forms
Yoga Sutras, 31, 112,
    113
yurt microcosm, 63, 64

zazen, 109: breathing in,
    109–10
Zeami, 135
Zen, 14, 20, 33, 53,
    73–4, 108–11